The Truman Years, 1945–1953

We work with leading authors to develop the
strongest educational materials in history,
bringing cutting-edge thinking and best learning
practice to a global market.

Under a range of well-known imprints, including
Longman, we craft high-quality print and electronic
publications which help readers to understand and
apply their content, whether studying or at work.

To find out more about the complete range of our
publishing please visit us on the World Wide Web at:
www.pearsoneduc.com

SEMINAR STUDIES IN HISTORY

The Truman Years, 1945–1953

MARK S. BYRNES

An imprint of **Pearson Education**

Harlow, England · London · New York · Reading, Massachusetts · San Francisco · Toronto · Don Mills, Ontario · Sydney
Tokyo · Singapore · Hong Kong · Seoul · Taipei · Cape Town · Madrid · Mexico City · Amsterdam · Munich · Paris · Milan

Pearson Education Limited
Edinburgh Gate
Harlow
Essex CM20 2JE
England
and Associated Companies throughout the world.

Visit us on the World Wide Web at:
www.pearsoneduc.com

First published 2000

© Pearson Education Limited 2000

ISBN 0-582-32904-3 PPR

British Library Cataloguing-in-Publication Data
A catalogue record for this book is
available from the British Library

Library of Congress Cataloging-in-Publication Data
Byrnes, Mark S. (Mark Stephen), 1961-
    The Truman years, 1945-1953 / Mark S. Byrnes.
        p. cm. -- (Seminar studies in history)
    Includes bibliographical references (p.) and index.
    ISBN 0-582-32904-3
    1. United States--Politics and government--1945-1953. 2. Truman, Harry S.,
    1884-1972. 3. United States--Foreign relations--1945-1953. 4. Cold War. I. Title. II.
    Series.

E813.B97 2001
973.918--dc21   00-034901

Set by 7 in 10/12 Sabon Roman
Printed in Malaysia, KVP

To the memory of Rosa F. Swartz, who showed me that teaching and learning know no age, time or place.

CONTENTS

AN INTRODUCTION TO THE SERIES

Such is the pace of historical enquiry in the modern world that there is an ever-widening gap between the specialist article or monograph, incorporating the results of current research, and general surveys, which inevitably become out of date. Seminar Studies in History are designed to bridge this gap. The series was founded by Patrick Richardson in 1966 and his aim was to cover major themes in British, European and World history. Between 1980 and 1996 Roger Lockyer continued his work, before handing the editorship over to Clive Emsley and Gordon Martel. Clive Emsley is Professor of History at the Open University, while Gordon Martel is Professor of International History at the University of Northern British Columbia, Canada and Senior Research Fellow at De Montfort University.

All the books are written by experts in their field who are not only familiar with the latest research but have often contributed to it. They are frequently revised, in order to take account of new information and interpretations. They provide a selection of documents to illustrate major themes and provoke discussion, and also a guide to further reading. The aim of *Seminar Studies* is to clarify complex issues without over-simplifying them, and to stimulate readers into deepening their knowledge and understanding of major themes and topics.

NOTE ON REFERENCING SYSTEM

Readers should note that numbers in square brackets [5] refer them to the corresponding entry in the Bibliography at the end of the book (specific page numbers are given in italics). A number in square brackets preceded by *Doc.* [*Doc. 5*] refers readers to the corresponding item in the Documents section which follows the main text. Asterisks mark terms that can be found in the Glossary.

AUTHOR'S ACKNOWLEDGEMENTS

I would like to thank Gordon Martel for offering me the opportunity to write this book, my mentor Robert A. Divine for being living proof that one can be a serious scholar and still write clearly for a wider audience, and my friend John Koskoski for reading the manuscript and offering useful comments.

PUBLISHER'S ACKNOWLEDGEMENTS

We are indebted to Houghton Mifflin Inc. for permission to quote their *Major Problems in American History since 1945*, ed. Robert Griffith, published by D.C. Heath, 1992, as a reference source. We are grateful to Popperfoto for permission to reproduce the cover image of Harry S. Truman holding the *Chicago Tribune* and for Plates 1, 2, 3 and 4.

LIST OF ABBREVIATIONS

ADA	Americans for Democratic Action
AMA	American Medical Association
CCP	Chinese Communist Party
CIA	Central Intelligence Agency
CIO	Congress of Industrial Organizations
CPUS	Communist Party of the United States
ERA	Equal Rights Amendment
ERP	European Recovery Program (Marshall Plan)
FBI	Federal Bureau of Investigation
FDR	Franklin D. Roosevelt
FEPC	Fair Employment Practices Commission
GOP	Grand Old Party (Republican Party)
HUAC	House Committee on Un-American Activities
IMF	International Monetary Fund
NAACP	National Association for the Advancement of Colored People
NATO	North Atlantic Treaty Organization
NSA	National Security Act of 1947
NSC	National Security Council
NSC-68	National Security Council Paper No. 68
OSS	Office of Strategic Services
OWI	Office of War Information
TVA	Tennessee Valley Authority
UMW	United Mine Workers
UNSC	United Nations Security Council
WFTU	World Federation of Trade Unions
WPA	Works Progress Administration

N

NORWAY

SWEDEN

DENMARK

GREAT
BRITAIN

Hamburg
London   NETHERLANDS
ENGLISH CHANNEL
BELGIUM   Bonn
Frankfurt
Paris   LUX.
W.
GERMANY

Berlin
E.
GERMANY

POLAND

Warsaw

CZECHOSLOVAKIA

Vienna

Budapest
HUNGARY

SWITZ.   AUSTRIA

FRANCE

ITLAY

Belgrade

YUGLOSLAVIA

PORTUGAL

Madrid

SPAIN

Rome

*Communist
activity 1946–49*

Map 1   Cold war Europe, 1946

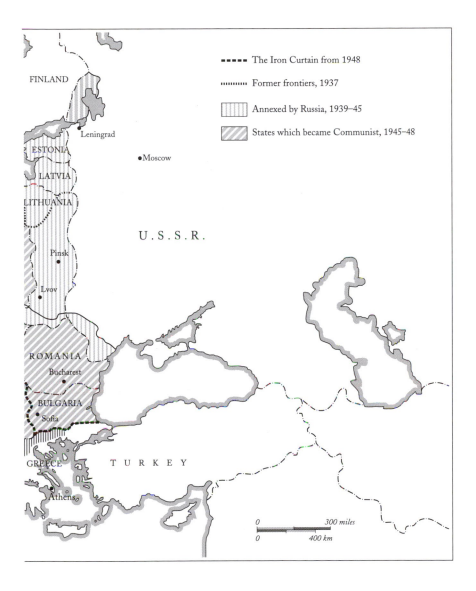

The Iron Curtain from 1948

Former frontiers, 1937

Annexed by Russia, 1939–45

States which became Communist, 1945–48

FINLAND

Leningrad

ESTONIA

LATVIA

LITHUANIA

•Moscow

U.S.S.R.

Pinsk

Lvov

ROMANIA

Bucharest

BULGARIA

Sofia

GREECE

TURKEY

Athens

0   300 miles

0   400 km

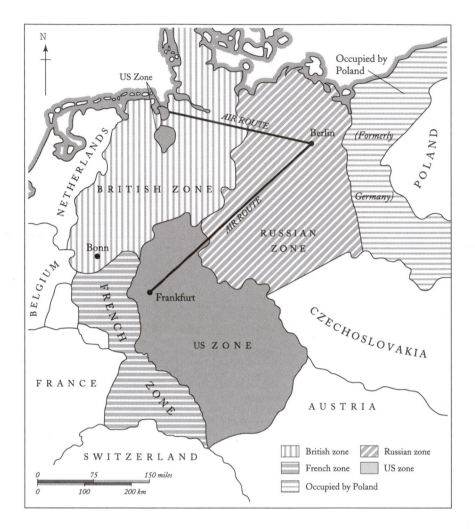

Map 2   Cold war Germany, 1946

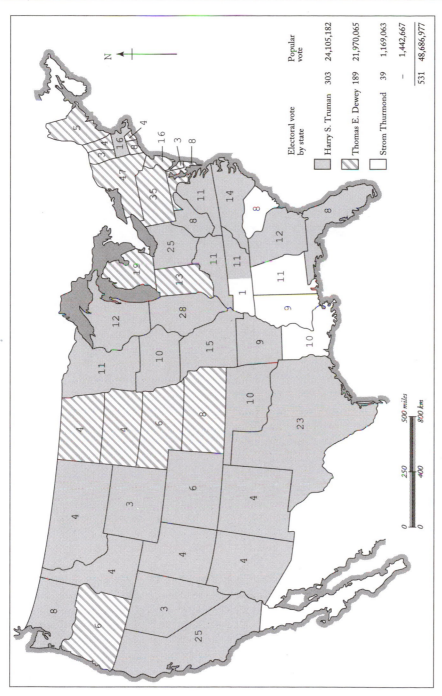

Map 3   The 1948 election results

CHAPTER ONE

INTRODUCTION: THE UNITED STATES IN 1945

It is rare when a single year emerges as a clear line between historical eras. It is even more rare when that year coincides with a particular presidential administration. Yet such is the case with 1945. Perhaps only 1865, with the nearly simultaneous death of Abraham Lincoln and the end of the Civil War, rivals 1945 as a clearly defined turning point in American history. The death of Franklin Roosevelt came only weeks before the end of the war in Europe, and months prior to the surrender of Japan. The burden of the tremendous shift from fighting the most destructive war in history to rebuilding the devastated battlegrounds of Europe and Asia fell on a relatively untested politician from Missouri, Harry S. Truman.

Franklin Roosevelt bequeathed to Harry Truman a nation far different from the one he inherited from Herbert Hoover in 1933. In that dark year, the United States was wallowing in the depths of the Great Depression. As war approached in Europe and Asia, the country turned inward, reverting to the reflexive isolationism which had dominated so much of its history. On the April day in 1945 when Harry Truman first took the oath of office, the United States was the dominant economic power in the world, and stood on the brink of military victories in both Europe and Asia, the leader of an international coalition against the fascist powers.

The transformation was nothing short of remarkable. The entire federal budget in 1939 was approximately $9 billion. In 1945, it was over $100 billion. The gross national product more than doubled during the war. With breathtaking speed, the United States had undergone a dramatic evolution, but the future remained obscure. Would the price of peace be the disappearance of the prosperity of the war years? Would the American public, its adversaries abroad vanquished, return to its traditional aversion to involvement in European affairs? Over the next nearly eight years, Truman would preside over the creation of both the postwar world and postwar America. The Truman administration was a formative time, when the tremendous forces unleashed during World War II would take on concrete expression, an era in which patterns were established in both domestic and world politics which would mark the United States for the rest of the century.

Their confidence first shaken by the deprivation and want of the 1930s, and then restored by triumph in war, Americans were simultaneously secure and fearful in 1945. They had greater power, greater wealth than ever before. They also had more to lose than ever before, and a haunting sense of how easily it might all vanish. The stock market crash of 1929 and subsequent downward spiral of the economy had shown that great prosperity could be fleeting. The shocking Japanese attack on Pearl Harbor removed the illusion that the United States was invulnerable behind the mighty natural defenses of the Atlantic and Pacific Oceans. Even the awesome power that helped end the war was cause for deep concern: how safe was anyone in a world in which a city could disappear in a flash?

The most obvious and immediate burden facing Truman was of course the end of World War II. It was nonetheless one of the least of the challenges the former farmer and failed haberdasher faced in his presidency. The war was nearly over in Europe; Germany's collapse was expected soon. While the future looked more ominous in the Asian theater, within three months, Truman would receive the news of the successful testing of the atomic bomb; a month later, the Japanese would surrender.

Far more daunting and intractable were the problems of peace. In foreign affairs, the final defeat of the Axis produced no utopian paradise. The destruction and consequent misery produced by the war would take years to overcome. The wartime alliance with the Soviet Union slowly disintegrated, producing a new sense of danger in the world, a new dragon to slay. In the aftermath of the war effort, many Americans seemed to yearn to return to a simpler time and their traditional isolation from political involvement in world affairs.

Even the more pleasant prospect of a prosperous life at home was not without qualification. Yes, the massive government spending of the war had finally ended the Great Depression. But the new-found wealth of the nation seemed precarious to many Americans. Would the prosperity which came during the war survive during the peace? What was the best way to ensure that it did: continuing New Deal/wartime-style management of the economy, or a return to a more *laissez-faire* approach now that the economic and military crisis had passed? How did one convert an economy geared to war production back to civilian purposes without massive disruption? Where would the millions of servicemen find work once they returned home from the war?

Perhaps even more profound than these immediate economic concerns were the ramifications of the social changes the previous years of depression and war had wrought on American society. The humiliation many men felt at the inability to perform their traditional role as provider in the Depression had taken a toll on patriarchy. The imperatives of war production had pressed millions of women into new, previously unthinkable, lines of work and had begun to erode the entrenched view of the proper place of women. A similar dynamic was transforming race relations. Millions of African-American men and women, who served their country in uniform or in the factories, would find it increasingly difficult to accept the second-class citizenship of the Jim Crow segregation* of the South and the *de facto* discrimination of the North. The disruptions of the Depression and the war undermined the family as a unit of social stability, foreshadowing the youth rebellion of the 1960s.

It fell to Harry Truman to lead and manage these profound political, economic and social changes. Truman made no bones about his sense that he was not up to the task. He confessed to his diary that he felt 'shocked when I was told of the President's death and the weight of the Government had fallen on my shoulders' [*Doc. 1*]. In many ways, however, Harry Truman was no accidental president. The fact that the former senator from Missouri was in line to become president was not the product of presidential or party whim. It was a calculated decision, one which reflected the changing mood and needs of the nation. Truman was a New Dealer who was uncomfortable with some of the 'professional liberals' who were drawn to Franklin D. Roosevelt (FDR). He was a parochial man from the Midwest who had never left the United States prior to his service in World War I, yet drew from that experience and his reading in history an appreciation for the more cosmopolitan world-view of the eastern establishment.

Even temperamentally, Truman was well-suited to his time. Lacking both the dour stoicism of Herbert Hoover and the ebullient optimism of Franklin Roosevelt, Truman reflected the ambivalence of his age. As many contemporary commentators and subsequent biographers have noted, Truman's scrappy, decisive image sometimes concealed a deep-seated insecurity and sense of inferiority. Like the nation he led, Truman could be both cocky and paranoid, generous and petty, visionary and parochial. He was a man raised on nineteenth-century values thrust suddenly into the leadership of a rapidly changing twentieth-century nation. If he often fumbled and stumbled in his effort to reconcile this new world with the quite different one which produced him, many Americans no doubt saw in that struggle a reflection of their own bewilderment at how quickly their world had changed around them.

In that *ad hoc* improvising which marked much of Truman's presidency, however, the contours of postwar America were established: a *status quo* politics that both accepted the basic outlines of the limited welfare state which was the legacy of FDR's New Deal, and resisted its expansion; an internationalist world-view which assumed the necessity of American leadership, defined increasingly by the cold war struggle with the Soviet Union; an evolving transformation of race and gender roles in American society. Overall, the Truman years were a time of transition and transformation, as the United States adjusted to events at home and abroad which dramatically changed the nature of American government, society and diplomacy.

PART ONE

YEARS OF UNCERTAINTY, 1945–46

CHAPTER TWO

THE DECISION TO DROP THE ATOMIC BOMB

One of the momentous events that marks the year 1945 as a turning point, not only in American but in world history, is the advent of the atomic weapons. In August, the United States dropped two atomic bombs on Japan, the first (and thus far only) use of nuclear devices in combat. For the first time in history, the human race faced the prospect of complete annihilation. Nothing would ever be quite the same again.

Harry Truman always maintained that once he made the decision to use the atomic bomb, he never gave it a second thought. If that is true (and there is some reason to doubt that it is), the president was the only one who considered the subject closed. The controversy over Truman's decision has continued ever since. It was perhaps the most significant decision that Truman ever made, with far-reaching consequences, and it is still hotly debated more than 50 years later [18; 63; 91].

ENDING THE WAR IN ASIA

Bringing World War II to a quick, successful conclusion was the most pressing matter the new president faced. In Europe, it was only a matter of time. Allied forces were closing on Berlin from east and west, and Germany would surrender less than a month into Truman's presidency. The Asian theater was another matter entirely. The tortuous process of approaching Japan through the island-hopping campaign was slow and brutal. Truman's first weeks as president coincided with the battle for Okinawa, which lasted until June. The battle saw 16 US ships sunk (and another 185 damaged) by Japanese kamikaze suicide attacks. Apart from the actual damage done, the kamikaze attacks created the impression of a fanatical resistance by the Japanese which could only be overcome at great cost. At the time of the German surrender, V-E Day, 8 May 1945, American political and military leaders feared that the war with Japan might go on another 12–18 months. Preliminary plans called for a potential invasion of the Japanese home islands in 1946 [16; 142].

On the diplomatic front, the United States had long been pushing the Soviet Union to enter the war against Japan, which they agreed to do at the Yalta Conference* in February 1945. According to the agreement, the Soviets were to enter the Asian war three months from the end of the war in Europe. The United States hoped that the general desperation of the Japanese position, combined with the Soviet entry, would bring an end to the war without the necessity of an invasion of the Japanese home islands, which everyone assumed would exact a high cost in lives lost – tens of thousands at least. After meeting with Stalin at the Potsdam Conference* on 17 July, Truman noted in his diary that the Soviets would be in the war by 15 August. 'Fini Japs when that comes about,' Truman wrote [5 *p. 53*].

The successful testing of an atomic device at Alamogordo, New Mexico on 16 July 1945, raised another possibility: atomic strikes on Japanese cities which would force an early surrender. Despite the later controversy over the decision, there seems to have been little hesitancy on Truman's part, and little vocal dissent among the upper reaches of policy-making. The Interim Committee, appointed by Truman to make recommendations regarding the use of the weapon, had recommended in May 1945 that the bomb be used without warning against a 'vital war plant employing a large number of workers and closely surrounded by workers' houses.' The purpose, they concluded, was to 'make a profound psychological impression on as many of the inhabitants as possible.' A group of atomic scientists who worked on the project advised against 'an early unannounced attack against Japan.' The chances of controlling a potential arms race would be increased, they argued, by a demonstration in an uninhabited area. The government's scientific advisory committee rejected that idea, concluding that 'we see no acceptable alternative to direct military use.' With near unanimity among his top advisors, Truman quickly decided to use the bomb against Japan at the earliest practical date [51 *pp. 51–4*].

THE DEBATE

The controversy over Truman's decision revolves around the question of whether using the bomb was truly necessary to achieve a quick surrender by the Japanese. Critics have argued that Japan was looking for a way to surrender, but the Truman administration, eager to demonstrate the power of its new weapon to the world (the Soviets in particular), ignored that possibility. They point out that the US Strategic Bombing Survey concluded in 1946 that Japanese surrender was likely before the end of 1945, perhaps even by 1 November, even without the use of the bomb, Soviet entry into the war, or the prospect of a US invasion. Others have suggested that revenge for Pearl

Harbor (polls showed that 75 percent of the public approved of the bombing), racism, and bureaucratic momentum all contributed to the unnecessary use of the atom bomb [17].

Truman's defenders have noted that American (and Allied) policy was unconditional surrender, and there was little or no indication that the Japanese were willing to accept that outcome before the use of the bomb. They cite various estimates of possible American casualties in an assault on the Japanese main islands, ranging from tens of thousands to hundreds of thousands, and argue that it would have been unconscionable for Truman not to use the bomb if it held the possibility of preventing such a calamity. Perhaps the war might have ended soon without the use of the bomb, but no one could know that with any certainty in August 1945, and in the meantime, additional American lives would have been lost while the war continued [72; 91].

The debate has been one of the most heated in American history, perhaps because the stakes are so large. If the use of the atomic bomb was truly unnecessary, then Harry Truman needlessly and deliberately massacred hundreds of thousands of civilians, and launched a nuclear arms race which had the potential to eradicate life on earth, all for a short-term advantage in the coming cold war, or for personal political benefit. If, on the other hand, the use of the bomb was necessary, then Truman's critics have unfairly leveled the most serious charges against an innocent man who merely sought, as any responsible leader would, to end the war as quickly as possible with as little loss of life among his own people as possible.

Given the emotional nature of such a debate, there is no overall consensus on the subject. Still, most students of the subject (though not all) reject the idea that Truman *knew* the bombing was unnecessary to produce surrender and ordered it anyway. Undeniably, Truman's critics have made valid points which even his most staunch defenders will concede. For example, few historians would deny that Truman and some of his advisors hoped that the bomb would produce diplomatic benefits in the postwar world, particularly in dealing with the Soviet Union, even if it was not the reason for the bombing. Secretary of State James F. Byrnes commented to Truman that possession of the bomb would give the United States an edge in postwar negotiations, and Truman evidently agreed. It is important to note, however, that it was the mere *possession* of the bomb which was seen as giving the United States an edge. Certainly the use of the bomb would add to that advantage, but that does not necessarily mean that Truman dropped the bomb to impress the Soviets.

Also, it does seem indisputable that Truman made little attempt to seek a less than unconditional surrender from the Japanese. One of the strongest arguments which the critics make is that the Japanese would have surrendered had they been assured in advance that they could keep the emperor (a concession which the United States granted *after* their unconditional surrender). By failing to test this possibility, they argue, Truman missed an opportunity to avoid the necessity of using this terrible weapon. Nonetheless, in insisting on unconditional surrender, Truman was merely maintaining the policy announced by FDR years before. It is perhaps a bit unfair to expect that a new president overrule the established policy of his predecessor only months into his administration, particularly when there was no guarantee that it would produce results, and it was possible that the Japanese might see the concession as an invitation to bargain further for even better terms.

What is undeniable is that the use of the atomic bomb was followed quickly by the Japanese surrender. The intervention of Emperor Hirohito tipped the divided Japanese government in favor of surrender. The fact that the Japanese military wanted to fight on despite the destruction of Hiroshima and Nagasaki (as well as the Soviet declaration of war) is perhaps the strongest evidence that Japan was unlikely to give up the fight without the horrible devastation of the atom bomb. However necessary the use of the atomic bomb may have been, the most destructive force known to man had been unleashed. The mushroom clouds over Japan would cast a disturbing and permanent shadow over the entire world.

CHAPTER THREE

FROM CO-OPERATION TO CONFRONTATION

The Truman administration's obvious concern with the Soviet Union high-lights the other important foreign policy consideration of the early Truman years. Truman inherited an increasingly difficult relationship with the Soviets from FDR. As the wartime necessity of co-operation began to wane with the decline and fall of the Nazi regime, the divergent interests of the two allies increasingly came to the fore. FDR's hopes for a stable postwar environment hinged on the ability of the United States and the Soviet Union to co-operate in managing the new world order. He recognized that the two nations, so different in history, ideology, and geography, would not see eye to eye on every issue. For example, while FDR knew that he could not prevent the Soviets from establishing a sphere of influence in eastern Europe, he remained optimistic that good relations between the United States and the Soviet Union could ameliorate the impact of the Soviet sphere. If the Soviets used restraint and were not too heavy-handed in their domination, it would not prove problematic. In practice, however, the Soviet Union proved insensitive to American concerns, especially those of the American public. FDR went to his grave hopeful that the mutual interest of the great powers in preventing another cataclysmic world war would allow them to continue the co-operation of the war years to their common benefit. It was not to be.

WHEN DID THE COLD WAR BEGIN?

Precisely when the 'cold war' began has also been a subject of much controversy. Historians have proposed various starting dates, from the Bolshevik Revolution* in 1917, to the dropping of the atomic bombs in 1945, to Churchill's 'Iron Curtain' speech* [Doc. 6] and Stalin's election speech in 1946, to the announcement of the Truman Doctrine* in 1947 [Doc. 8]. While each has a certain merit, the mere variety of dates suggests a more basic truth about the cold war. Unlike an actual war, the cold war was never a direct confrontation between the United States and the Soviet Union on a battlefield. Instead it was an intense competition stretching over decades, in which the two adversaries jockeyed for position *vis-à-vis* each other short of war. The use of the term 'cold *war*' has often led observers to think in terms of a starting date. While the cold war often did take on some of the attributes of an actual conflict, in this case the term is misleading. The cold war was a relationship, and had no precise beginning; it evolved. It is therefore more accurate to think in terms of a process, rather than a discrete event. (Its end is similarly controversial and gradual.)

The desire to find a precise date for the start of the cold war has led some to focus on Truman himself [17]. If the cold war was an abrupt shift in policy, then it perhaps follows that it resulted from the abrupt change in leadership. According to this view, the replacement of the more seasoned, cosmopolitan FDR with the inexperienced, more blunt man from Missouri was the crucial event which led to the cold war. No one can say for certain how FDR would have dealt with the Soviets after World War II. Certainly he would have tried to continue to get along with the Soviets, but would he have been able to maintain a co-operative relationship in the face of the changing international realities which Truman faced? After all, Truman also tried to keep on good terms with the Soviets.

It is true that Truman's experiences in the early months of his presidency led him to doubt the feasibility of FDR's optimistic vision. In his view (and that of many of the advisors he inherited from FDR, such as Admiral William Leahy and Ambassador Averill Harriman), Soviet behaviour in eastern Europe at the end of the war did not bode well for future co-operation. The Soviets were intent on installing regimes friendly to themselves in the nations which the Red Army liberated from the Nazis. While their actions could be seen as consistent with a simple desire for security against a resurgent Germany, Truman and others in the administration saw them as far more ominous. He feared that unless they were faced with firm resistance, Soviet ambitions would become as unlimited and dangerous as those of Hitler. Still, Truman did not immediately abandon hopes of co-operation with the Soviets.

THE ROOTS OF THE COLD WAR

One should not overestimate the importance of Truman's personal views. The president's concerns were not only his own, nor were they based only on recent events. Long-standing American suspicions of the Soviet regime created the context in which American leaders saw Soviet postwar actions. Ever since Lenin and the Bolsheviks came to power in 1917, hostility and fear had been far more common than co-operation in US–Soviet relations. Prompted by the British and French, President Woodrow Wilson joined the other Allied powers in sending 7,000 troops into the Soviet Union in 1918 to try to crush the revolution in its infancy. Although that effort failed, the United States expressed its revulsion at the Soviet system by refusing to recognize Lenin's government. The Soviet Union's call for world revolution was seen as a threat to the democratic capitalist system in the United States, and there were no formal relations between the two states from 1917 to 1933.

FDR's 1933 decision to grant diplomatic recognition to the Soviet regime (in hopes of both opening new markets in the midst of the Great Depression, and balancing the growing power of Japan in Asia) did not lead to cordial relations in the 1930s. The Nazi–Soviet non-aggression pact of 1939 caused a surge of anti-communism in the United States. Even in the midst of the common fight against Hitler, FDR decided not to inform the Soviets officially of the secret Manhattan Project* to build the atomic bomb. In short, long before the end of World War II, Americans viewed the Soviets with deep suspicion.

Thus, when the Soviets appeared to be taking advantage of the chaotic situation in Europe at the end of the war, the pro-Soviet view taken by American leaders during the dark days of the war quickly evaporated. Truman served notice that he would not stand by while the Soviets, in his view, violated their agreements with the United States. In his first meeting with a high-ranking Soviet official, Foreign Minister V. Molotov on 23 April 1945, Truman, according to several accounts, gave the Soviet leader a stern talking to, warning him that the United States expected the Soviet Union to live up to its agreements [9 *p. 82*]. The significance of Truman's tough talk should not be exaggerated, however. Shortly after his confrontation with Molotov, in June 1945, Truman sent FDR's trusted aide Harry Hopkins to Moscow to smooth things over with Stalin regarding Poland. Truman still thought he needed the Soviets for the war against Japan, the same factor that guided FDR's policy of accommodation. Truman did not, however, believe that the relationship could work unless the Soviets knew that the United States would continue steadfastly to defend its own interests. Truman went to the Potsdam Conference in July 1945 still seeing himself as a mediator between Churchill and Stalin.

For most of the first two years of his presidency, Truman's approach to the Soviet Union was marked by this ambivalent attitude. On the one hand, he sought to implement FDR's policy; for example, through the establishment of the United Nations, with its Security Council composed of great powers ensuring world peace. On the other hand, he was temperamentally and intellectually drawn to a no-nonsense, tough-talking approach which had the potential to make co-operation difficult if not impossible. Truman wavered between the two approaches before finally settling on a policy of ongoing confrontation in early 1947.

THE LEGACY OF WORLD WAR II

The postwar policies of both the United States and the Soviet Union are perhaps best viewed in the context of each nation's recent experiences in the 1930s and 1940s. Officials of the Truman administration took from the experience of the 1930s clear lessons: appeasement* of a dictator makes war more, not less, likely; economic nationalism in the form of high tariffs and other barriers to free trade impoverishes nations and provokes war. In addition, the attack on Pearl Harbor (the first meaningful attack on American territory by a foreign foe since the War of 1812) exposed US vulnerability and fostered a determination never to be caught napping again. Technology had made the world a smaller place, geography was no longer an adequate defense. In sum, these attitudes constituted a dramatic redefinition of American security. The peace and prosperity of the world were inextricably interwoven with the security and economic health of the United States. The leaders making American foreign policy after the war were committed internationalists, who firmly believed in the necessity of an ongoing American role in the world. In the postwar period, the Soviet Union was the only remaining power with the capacity to damage the United States, and American leaders were determined to be vigilant against any potential threat to ever-expanding American interests [84].

The Soviet leader Joseph Stalin also drew lessons from the 1930s. The appeasement of Hitler by the western powers and their refusal to ally with the Soviets in the 1930s was a symbol of intransigent western hostility to communism, which would not end until communism prevailed everywhere. Stalin's experience with Hitler also proved that treaties are no guarantee of security. Despite the Nazi–Soviet non-aggression pact of 1939, Hitler's armies invaded the Soviet Union in June 1941. The plains of Poland had proven too conducive to invasion and would need to be controlled by the Soviet Union. A united Germany, with its natural resources and educated populace, was naturally the most powerful nation in Europe and could not be allowed to rise and threaten the Soviet Union again. Only a powerful Soviet Union, with its weaker neighbors firmly under its control, would be safe.

Thus the ghost of Adolph Hitler hung over postwar Europe, not only in the physical destruction his megalomania produced, but in the fear and suspicion his actions produced in his former enemies. The memory of what he had so recently wrought reinforced pre-existing attitudes and created new suspicions. This combination of a power vacuum in Europe, two newly dominant yet insecure nations, and the dramatic ideological differences between them, combined to produce the intense international rivalry known as the cold war.

In the United States, the long-standing fear of communist ideology now fused with a potential military threat. Hopes for a peaceful postwar world increasingly gave way to fears of another aggressive totalitarian* system seeking to dominate Europe, with the potential for the same disastrous consequences so recently experienced. The war had taught Americans that the United States could not live in a world dominated by a totalitarian regime. Even if the United States were not attacked directly, its way of life would be ruined by such domination. American goods would be frozen out of foreign markets and American military forces would have to maintain a permanent war footing. The result would be significant strains on the American economy, high levels of taxation, and the regimentation of society in such a way as to destroy the American way of life. If co-operation were possible with the Soviet Union, it would have to be on American terms: democracy and free trade [84]. As Harry Truman himself put it when preparing for the Potsdam Conference in August 1945, the United States might not get all that it wanted in negotiations with the Soviets, but 'we should be able to get eighty-five percent' [85 *p. 47*].

Soviet motivations remain the subject of intense controversy, clouded in the secrecy of Stalin's totalitarian system. Even recent revelations from the Soviet archives have not ended the debates over Soviet intentions after World War II. This much is clear: Stalin ruled the Soviet Union with an iron fist, tolerating no dissent, ruthlessly crushing all opposition to his rule, real and imagined. His foreign policy aims are not quite as clear. Some historians see Stalin's diplomacy as marked by a cautious, realistic nationalism, primarily serving Soviet national interests in a prudent fashion, seeking to enhance Soviet security through control over nearby 'buffer' states. Others see a nascent Hitler, an ideologically-driven megalomaniac who desired to spread the Soviet system throughout Europe and the world, whose evil designs were only thwarted by the determination of the United States.

There can be no doubt that Stalin, at a minimum, was determined to re-establish the 1941 borders of the Soviet Union (thus including part of pre-war Poland as well as the Baltic states). He was just as intent on dominating eastern Europe. In a famous meeting with Churchill in October 1944, Stalin and the British prime minister agreed on a 'percentages deal,' in which the Soviets would have 90 percent of the influence in Rumania, 75 percent in Bulgaria, and 50 percent in Yugoslavia and Hungary [3 *p. 227*]. As subsequent events made clear, Stalin also was determined to control Poland. Beyond that, things get murky. Did Stalin have designs on all of Europe? Was he dedicated to communist revolution worldwide? Stalin was certainly opportunistic, and sought to extend Soviet power and influence as far as he reasonably could. However, he also demonstrated on numerous occasions the ability to reconcile himself to American interests, particularly when Americans asserted them strongly. Unlike Hitler in Poland, Stalin never launched an aggressive war to challenge an area of vital interest to the United States and the west. As a dedicated communist, Stalin apparently believed that eventually war between capitalism and communism was inevitable. But he was patient, and willing to wait. That does not mean that Stalin was not a potential threat to American interests. It does, however, suggest that he was a manageable threat.

Certainly Truman at first thought that Stalin could be managed. After meeting with him for the first time at Potsdam, Truman concluded that Stalin was a man who '[k]nows what he wants and will compromise when he can't get it' [54 p. 331]. Such a leader might be a difficult, but not impossible, postwar partner. Truman's expectations of getting most of what he wanted proved unrealistic, however. At Potsdam, disagreement over Germany (particularly the issue of reparations) exposed differences among the Allies. The United States was looking toward rebuilding a strong Germany to stabilize Europe, while the Soviets feared a revived Germany might once again present a real threat to the Soviet Union.

At the first Council of Foreign Ministers meeting in London in September 1945, the Soviets served notice that they were not going to be intimidated by the atomic bomb. As differences emerged and agreement grew unlikely, Foreign Minister Molotov sarcastically asked Secretary of State James F. Byrnes if he had an atomic bomb with him. Byrnes replied that he would 'pull an atomic bomb out of my hip pocket and let you have it' if the Soviets did not become more reasonable [64 p. 54]. The levity of the exchange could not hide the underlying reality: the atomic bomb was too blunt an instrument to be effective diplomatically. The United States was not about to drop the bomb on Moscow over any of the outstanding issues. The acrimony of the London conference left the powers suspicious of each other.

The next meeting, in Moscow in December 1945, produced results on eastern Europe, as the United States accepted the addition of token non-communists in their governments in lieu of free elections. In effect, it was a *de facto* recognition of a Soviet sphere. No progress was made on what would become a more vexing issue, however: the presence of Soviet troops in Iran. Truman grew increasingly concerned that Soviet policy indicated a pattern of aggression. They had tightened their grip on eastern Europe, and seemed poised to push for greater influence in southeastern Europe and the Middle East. Stalin's 9 February 1946 speech seemed to confirm Truman's worst fears. The Soviet leader spoke of the incompatibility of capitalism and communism; World War II, he said, grew inevitably out of the contradictions of capitalism, implying that another war would come with the next 'crisis' in the capitalist world. Soon after, the Soviet Union announced it would not participate in the American system for the international economic system, the International Monetary Fund (IMF) and the World Bank. Fearing capitalist infiltration, Stalin decided to forego these potential sources of the funds he needed to rebuild his ravaged country.

TOWARD CONTAINMENT*

In the United States, an emerging anti-Soviet consensus began to take shape. Two analyses of Soviet policy, one secret and the other public, reflected a growing concern over Soviet behaviour. The first was the famous 'Long Telegram'* from US State Department veteran, George F. Kennan [*Doc. 5*]. An experienced observer of the Soviets, Kennan was at the time serving in the American Embassy in Moscow. From his front-row seat, he described his view of Soviet intentions and the best American response to them. He saw Soviet policy as a combination of traditional Russian insecurity about the west and communist ideology. The sense of a threat from the west was used by the party to suppress dissent at home and justify an aggressive policy abroad. Their ideology taught them that there could be no long-term peace with the capitalist west, and that only by disrupting the United States and its allies could Soviet security be maintained. Kennan concluded that the United States must reorient its foreign policy to meet the Soviet challenge 'with [the] same thoroughness and care as [the] solution of [a] major strategic problem in war' [*Doc. 5*; 12 *p. 707*]. War would not be necessary, he argued, as long as the United States demonstrated its willingness to defend its interests. Only by firmly resisting Soviet advances could the west hope to modify Soviet behaviour. Kennan's telegram was widely circulated, and began to crystallize official American opinion about the Soviet Union. It diagnosed the sources of Soviet behaviour and prescribed a remedy.

A month later, former Prime Minister Winston Churchill came to Truman's home state and gave a public address which helped polarize American opinion. Speaking in Fulton, Missouri, with Truman sharing the dais, Churchill effectively called for an end to the Big Three alliance of the war years, to be replaced by an Anglo-American concert of power. In the well-known, dramatic highlight of the speech, he declared that 'an iron curtain has descended across the continent.' The nations of eastern Europe were now controlled by 'police governments,' while Greece, Turkey and Iran were under increasing pressure from the Soviets. Churchill no doubt spoke for many in the west when he concluded, 'this is certainly not the liberated Europe we fought to build up.' Churchill made expert use of his own personal history as a prophet, noting that he had warned about Hitler in the 1930s and no one had listened [*Doc. 6*]. Although Truman avoided a specific endorsement of the content of Churchill's speech, his presence and failure to differ clearly indicated agreement. Within weeks, the president's harder line toward the Soviets over the looming crisis in Iran gave eloquent testimony to the drift in his thinking.

Some historians have argued that it was the crisis over Iran that signaled the start of the cold war [81]. While Americans had objected to Soviet domination of eastern Europe, and tried to use diplomacy to ameliorate it, in fact the United States accepted the creation of a Soviet sphere by 1946. The United States realized that nothing short of war would convince the Soviets to allow truly free, democratic elections when such would bring to power anti-Soviet regimes in areas which the Kremlin considered essential to its security. Other areas, such as Iran, were another matter entirely.

The crisis in Iran, like the others, grew out of World War II. During the war, the British and the Soviets partitioned Iran to keep it out of German hands, agreeing that they would withdraw their forces within six months of the end of the war. Thus the deadline was 2 March 1946. British troops began leaving in January, but Soviet troops remained. On 1 March, just days before the 'Iron Curtain' speech, the Soviets declared that they would remain beyond the deadline. The Soviets were trying to use their position to force Iran to grant them greater oil concessions in northern Iran. The British and the Americans, their awareness of the military and economic importance of oil heightened by the late war, saw the Soviet decision as an attempt to expand its influence into the oil-rich Middle East. Truman instructed the embassy in Moscow to protest vigorously, while the administration steadfastly supported Iran. Faced with strong resistance, Stalin opted for a face-saving agreement with Iran, and withdrew his forces by mid-May.

Stalin's retreat from Iran seemed to support the views of both Kennan and Churchill. The Soviets would back down when faced with resolute opposition. Hardliners could take from this experience the lesson that the Soviets must be countered at every turn by firm resolve. Seen in another light, however, Stalin's decision shows an aversion to risk. His aims in Iran were not worth the enmity they were eliciting from the west, and he made a calculated decision to back down gracefully. Stalin might yet prove to be another Hitler, but the Iran crisis suggested that he was more cautious and patient than the Nazi dictator.

In the summer of 1946, the growing consensus within the administration took the form of the Clifford–Elsey report. Two of Truman's aides, Clark Clifford and George Elsey, canvassed senior administration officials, and concluded that the Soviets were bent on undermining the United States and its allies throughout the world. The report called for the US government to support all those resisting Soviet pressure and/or aggression. It also went a step beyond Kennan and Churchill, arguing that the Soviets 'might at any time embark on a course of expansion effected by open warfare' [54 *p. 354*]. At the time, Truman considered the report too explosive and ordered that all copies be locked away; but in less than a year, Truman would publicly address Congress in similar terms in announcing the doctrine which bears his name.

Within the administration, only one voice of dissent remained: Commerce Secretary Henry Wallace. To many New Deal liberals, Wallace was the true heir to FDR, particularly in foreign policy. He had been FDR's vice-president during the war, and would have been president had he remained on the ticket in 1944. Long after others began to doubt the viability of FDR's vision of postwar co-operation with the Soviets, Wallace continued to argue that American obstinacy was the main impediment to good relations. Unlike most of the men around Truman, Wallace was suspicious of British motives. He suspected that Churchill's Fulton speech was meant to enlist the United States in a crusade, not for freedom, but to prop up Britain's declining imperial power [157; 161].

Although it was outside his official purview, Wallace sought to change the drift of American foreign policy. In a 23 July 1946 letter to the president, Wallace wrote that he was 'increasingly disturbed about the trend of international affairs' and the growing sense that another war was in the making. Describing American actions since the end of the war, Wallace saw a militarism that 'must make it look to the rest of the world that we are paying lip service to peace.' He called for a greater sensitivity to legitimate Russian security concerns, and an understanding that American actions must appear threatening to the Russians. The United States must adjust its thinking and 'recognize that the world has changed and there can be no "One World" unless the United States and Russia can find some way of living together' [*Doc. 7*].

Although Truman was clearly moving away from this line of thought, he had not abandoned it entirely and thus tolerated Wallace's dissent, perhaps hoping to avoid alienating liberals before the fall 1946 elections. When Wallace asked for Truman's approval of a foreign policy speech the Secretary was to give to a left-liberal meeting in Madison Square Garden in New York on 12 September, Truman hastily skimmed and approved it. In his address, Wallace explicitly accepted the Soviet sphere in eastern Europe, just as Secretary of State Byrnes was trying to get the Soviets to allow for greater democracy at the Foreign Ministers Conference in Paris. The result was public confusion over the true nature of the administration's policy. Byrnes demanded that Truman disown Wallace's statements, which was hard given the fact that Truman had publicly endorsed them. After a week of embarrassing attempts to finesse the situation, Truman asked for Wallace's resignation.

With the departure of Henry Wallace from the administration in September 1946, opponents of the emerging cold war consensus were few and far between. Nonetheless, Truman himself had not fully given up on a normal (though not particularly friendly) relationship with the Soviets. As Alonzo Hamby points out, the day after he fired Wallace, Truman optimistically wrote to another former vice-president, John Nance Gardner, that the United States was 'not going to have any shooting trouble' with the Russians. They are 'tough bargainers,' he said, but he expected that 'from now on we will have smoother sailing' [54 *p. 359*]. When the waters instead grew more troubled in the months ahead, Truman would finally join the growing chorus calling for confrontation with the Soviets.

CHAPTER FOUR

THE TRIALS OF RECONVERSION

Just as Harry Truman presided over the creation of a new American attitude toward the world, he also presided over the American government at a time in which American society was undergoing tremendous transformations. So much had changed in the last decade and a half. The United States had gone from the depths of the worst depression in its history to unprecedented heights of prosperity. The small-government philosophy which had dominated American attitudes since the American Revolution had been shaken by the dual impact of economic calamity and world war, which had increased both the size and the responsibilities of the federal government. The Depression and in particular the world war had accelerated social changes and dramatically altered the social landscape. How would the nation deal with the transformation back to a more normal lifestyle? More significantly, would life ever really be 'normal' again, after the fundamental alterations the country had experienced?

THE CHANGING ROLE OF WOMEN

Perhaps the largest and most far-reaching potential change was in the role of women. The need for American industry to increase its production just as millions of men were entering the armed forces necessitated a great departure – American women were encouraged to enter the work force in large numbers, and not just in the traditional roles of teacher, nurse, and secretary. At the encouragement of the Office of War Information (OWI), over six million women went to work. The public approved, as long as it was understood that this was a temporary crisis measure only.

Regardless of the stated intent, the fact that millions of women spent years during the war performing well at jobs which had always been considered the province of men was bound to have an impact on how Americans, particularly American women, thought about sex roles. The earlier growth of women in the work place that occurred in the 1920s had been interrupted abruptly by the Great Depression – with millions of men out of work, the public overwhelmingly disapproved of women taking jobs away from traditional male breadwinners. With the economy now healthy again, how would working women be perceived?

The key to understanding the short-range postwar mentality lies in two basic facts: (1) for most Americans (including working women), the war years were an aberration, not the new norm. Many of the women looked forward to returning to their traditional roles of wife and mother after the war. They did not see themselves as pioneers for equality of the sexes. (2) Although the United States was enjoying a wartime boom, fear of a postwar depression loomed. What would all of the returning veterans do for a living? If there were not enough jobs to go around, the assumption was that women would once again bow out so that men could return to their traditional role as primary wage earners for their families. While the reality of the war had shown that women *could* do many of the jobs traditionally done by men, it had failed to convert most Americans to the idea that women *should* do such jobs under normal circumstances.

The attitudes of Americans were not dramatically altered in the short run. A poll conducted in 1945 showed that 63 percent disapproved of wives working if their husbands could support the family [120 *p. 34*]. Unlike Europe, where the labor of women was essential to rebuild from the tremendous damage done by the war, American conditions were such that it was no longer necessary for women to work, and their continuing to work could reduce the opportunities for returning veterans. In such a climate, most women understandably went back to the domestic ideal. Many women returned voluntarily, while many others were fired from their jobs in war industries, at a rate far higher than that of men.

The economic impetus for a return to traditional roles was reinforced by a larger cultural concern for the state of the American family. Fifteen years of depression and war had taken a toll on the stability of the family. Increasingly, it seemed that children were breaking loose from parental authority. Social pressure enforced a return to the traditional domestic ideal [98].

The Depression and war had also had the effect of reducing the birth rate in recent years. Couples had refrained from starting families, first for eco-nomic reasons, then due to the absence of men during the war. Peace presented the opportunity for millions of young couples finally to start their families, which they did in unprecedented numbers: marriage and birth rates both increased dramatically. The result was the 'baby boom*,' the bulge in births between 1945 and 1960, which created a generation of Americans whose impact on American society would be felt for decades to come.

Despite the dominant trend toward the reaffirmation of the traditional family, the underlying reality had changed. Millions of women had done what only years earlier would have been unthinkable. While most women returned home, others did not, and many more wanted to continue working.

Women began to call for political action and reform; for example, reviving the Equal Rights Amendment (ERA)* to the Constitution, which said 'Men and women shall have equal rights throughout the United States and every place subject to its jurisdiction.' It had first been proposed in 1923, and was approved by a majority in the Senate in 1946, but fell short of the necessary two-thirds vote. The House never voted on it.

Other women demanded that action be taken to make it possible for women both to have careers and be mothers, just as men did not have to choose between their careers and fatherhood. In the more conservative political climate of the postwar era, however, calls for government-subsidized daycare were ignored. Despite these setbacks, signs of the changes wrought during the war were not long in coming. Although the number of women working dropped precipitously immediately after the war, the numbers began to go up again in the late 1940s, so much so that by 1950 the percentage of women working was greater than it had been in 1940, before the war, although not as high as its wartime peak. By 1955, the total number of women working exceeded the wartime high, both in raw numbers and in percentage of the work force.

While the influx of women into factories was portrayed as an aberration made necessary by the extreme emergency of total war, it was inevitable that the experience would undermine traditional gender roles. If women could ably do such jobs in an emergency, why should they be denied them in more tranquil times? Clearly, it was not a matter of ability, but of social convention. The seeds of the modern women's movement had been planted and would flower later in the 1960s and 1970s.

FORESHADOWING THE CIVIL RIGHTS MOVEMENT

The war also brought about other changes which would have a more immediate impact on American society. The enormous demand for labor not only brought more women into the work force, but also drew huge numbers of Americans from rural areas into cities, particularly African-Americans from the rural south to the industrial cities of the north [86]. Between 1940 and 1950, over two million African-Americans left the south for new opportunities in the north. In that same time period, 43 cities outside the South doubled their black population. While the nonwhite population of central cities was only 10 percent in 1940, it was over 33 percent in 1950. Despite the progress of the war years, economic disparities continued. Among minority families, over 51 percent had yearly incomes under $3,000 (in 1971 dollars) as compared to only 18.4 percent of white families. Median family income for minorities was half of that of white families.

Although the incentive to relocate to the north was usually an economic one, it also had profound political consequences. Those who left the old

Confederacy also left behind Jim Crow segregation and the myriad impediments to voting which arose in the late nineteenth century. The poll tax, literacy tests, the grandfather clause (which denied the vote to anyone whose grandfather could not vote, thus excluding all former slaves) and the terror tactics of groups like the Ku Klux Klan had effectively disenfranchised most southern blacks, nullifying the Fifteenth Amendment. Such obstacles to voting did not exist in the north. As a result, hundreds of thousands of newly enfranchised African-Americans in northern cities became a new constituency which political leaders increasingly courted in the postwar years [*Doc. 11*]. Previously, both major political parties could ignore black concerns, confident that they would suffer no adverse political consequences. With black voters now sending black representatives to Congress, or making the difference in close elections, they were gaining the political power to force their issues into the national political dialogue. This development became the political foundation for the nascent civil rights movement which would burst forth in the 1950s and 1960s.

Although the newcomers to the north usually met less resistance in registering to vote, they found no paradise there. During the war, the influx of blacks created racial tensions which sometimes spilled over into violence, such as the Detroit riot in the spring of 1943 and the riot in Harlem that August, which killed five people, injured 400, and caused $5 million in property damage. Segregation was a matter of law in the south; it was usually a matter of custom and tacit agreement in the north [149]. Housing was usually the problem, leading often to *de facto* segregation due to restrictive covenants, in which white owners agreed not to sell to black buyers. Despite the fact that the Supreme Court ruled in *Shelly v. Kramer* (1948)* that state courts could not enforce restrictive clauses in private contracts, the practice continued informally, making real integration of northern neighborhoods slow. And no legislation could prevent the white flight to the suburbs which often followed the arrival of large numbers of black Americans in the cities. This problem would pale in comparison to the challenge of *de jure* segregation and discrimination in the south, which would consume the energies of the civil rights movement, but would remain a serious problem whose true dimensions would emerge with a vengeance in the riots of the late 1960s in northern cities like Newark.

The war years also had an incalculable impact on the psychology of African-Americans, the scope of which became apparent during the Truman years. Over one million blacks were in uniform during the war, about 16 percent of the total (far greater than their 10 percent of the overall population). Although they served in segregated units during the war (FDR and the Joint Chiefs of Staff rejected the calls for integration with the argument that wartime is no time for social experimentation), these men who had served their country would not be likely to accept the second-class citizenship to which they had been consigned by America's history of racism and bigotry. Even during the war, the National Association for the Advancement of Colored People (NAACP)* had called for a 'double victory' over America's enemies abroad and racism at home. They attacked the hypocrisy of a nation which made war on Hitler's racist regime and yet tolerated segregation laws based on similar racist assumptions. The war had served the purpose of making even clearer the stark contradiction between American principles and American realities when it came to race. More blacks registered to vote during the war, even in the south, despite the terror used to discourage them. NAACP membership went from 50,000 to 450,000 during the war, promising a greater push for racial equality in the postwar years.

FDR's administration began a significant shift in the attitude of the Democratic Party toward civil rights. Ever since the Civil War, the Democrats had been the party of the south. The New Deal brought many black voters to the Democratic Party. Programs such as the Works Progress Administration (WPA) banned racial discrimination, and gave jobs to African-Americans. Although FDR's critics argue that there was relatively little substance behind his reputation, the fact remains that many blacks believed that FDR, unlike other recent presidents, cared about them. He created the impression that the Democratic Party, or at least its liberal, activist wing, was sympathetic to civil rights concerns.

Somewhat surprisingly, Harry Truman took up that mantle and took it further than FDR had. Coming from a former slave state, and counting slave owners among his ancestors, Truman's bona fides on civil rights might have been questionable. As president, Truman slowly moved beyond the prejudices of his youth. He was particularly sensitive to the abuses suffered by returning servicemen. Truman, who grew up with the racial attitudes typical of late nineteenth-century, small-town white Missouri, was particularly struck by stories of black servicemen being lynched upon their return to the United States. '[M]y very stomach turned over when I learned that Negro soldiers, just back from overseas, were being dumped out of Army trucks in Mississippi and beaten,' Truman wrote to a group of southern Democrats. 'Whatever my inclinations as a native of Missouri, as President I know this is bad. I shall fight to end evils like this' [103 *p. 588*].

Truman's sense of justice was appalled by the reality of Americans who had served their country in war being treated worse than animals. He proved sensitive to the changes which had taken place in recent years, both politically and socially. This combination of a new black militancy, created by participation in the war effort and a new demographic and political reality, was about to change the racial landscape in the United States in the first meaningful way since the Radical Republicans gave up on Reconstruction in the 1870s. While the first two years of his presidency saw little concrete action on civil rights, Truman would later emerge as an outspoken advocate of the cause, and take significant steps toward making the Democrats the party of African-Americans and civil rights.

REVERSALS FOR LABOR

Truman's initial domestic concerns were with reconversion from a wartime to a peacetime economy. One of the most wrenching problems had to do with the discontent of American workers, particularly labor unions. Labor had undergone a golden age in recent years. After struggling for recognition in the late nineteenth and early twentieth centuries, the New Deal finally granted government recognition and protection to labor with the Wagner Act of 1935. As a result, nearly 15 million Americans were in labor unions by 1945, about 35.8 percent of all nonagricultural workers. Nearly five times as many Americans were in labor unions as had been in 1933, a clear sign of the success of the New Deal in making organized labor an accepted part of the American economic and political system. But 1945 also marked the high water mark of American unionism. Its story for the rest of the century would be one of the slow erosion of labor's position, a deterioration which began in the Truman years.

Although wartime had seen an economic boom in the United States, the benefits had been somewhat limited for workers. Wage controls put a cap on how much unions could get from their employers at a time when labor shortages might otherwise have placed them in an ideal negotiating position. At the same time, union leaders saw their bosses gaining record profits, particularly those in the war industries. Generous government contracts guaranteed profits through the cost-plus system, which was meant to encourage speed over efficiency by insuring industries that their costs, no matter how high, would be covered by the government and would not cut into profits. The system produced incredible accelerations of production, and also enriched the businesses which received them.

It also changed the public image of business. In the 1930s, labor had benefited from the damage the Great Depression had done to the reputation of big business. The heroes of American prosperity in the 1920s, big businessmen, became the villains of the Depression in the 1930s. During the war, however, business had been rehabilitated and credited for the tremendous production which helped win the war. What was often over-looked was the fact that business benefited from generous tax breaks, the suspension of antitrust laws and a system which amounted to government subsidy. While the 'dollar-a-year' men served patriotically on government production boards, they often steered government contracts to their associates. The system certainly produced miracles, but it was hardly free enterprise. Nonetheless, business claimed and received credit for the economic boom [25].

Politically, the effect was the creation of a business–government partner-ship which left behind the rancor and class rhetoric of the New Deal 1930s. Both political parties saw co-operation with business as the way to ensure future prosperity, a theme which would dominate American politics after the war. The new image of business was patriotic and prosperity-producing. Meanwhile, the public saw labor's attempts to increase wages and gain a share of corporate decision-making as unpatriotic and power-hungry. Labor was also hurt by its left-wing associations and communist influence in some unions. Business adroitly and effectively exploited the opportunity to dis-credit unions, whose popularity suffered.

During the war, unions sought to lock in wage increases that would sus-tain the standard of living their members had come to enjoy. The attempt to do so led to assertive action, in the form of strikes. In 1943–44, record work stoppages had alienated even FDR, and had turned many Americans against labor. The last year of the war saw just as many work stoppages, and one million workers were on strike in January 1946. The labor agitation peaked in 1946, when one worker in 14 was out on strike at one point or another, potentially threatening a smooth transition to a peacetime economy. The unions were pushing for 30 percent wage increases, and got around 18 per-cent in major industries. In effect, business bought off workers with increased benefits, which unions now sought through negotiations with management because the conservative postwar political climate made it unlikely they would get them through government action.

Truman's attitude toward labor was marked by his usual ambivalence. In his first major domestic policy address to Congress in September, Truman said: 'This is not the time for short-sighted management to seize upon the chance to reduce wages and try to injure labor unions. Equally it is not the time for labor leaders to shirk their responsibility and permit widespread industrial strife' [*Doc. 3*]. In general, he was supportive of labor, but often had serious run-ins with labor leaders. Truman thought that the patriotic unity of purpose that was shown during the war should carry over into the postwar period, and was angered by the actions of strikers, particularly when he felt they threatened the national interest. In the spring of 1946, when 400,000 miners of the United Mine Workers (UMW) union went on strike, President Truman seized the mines and retained control when management refused to accept an agreement which the union had negotiated with the government.

A railroad strike followed in May, and when federal mediation failed to satisfy the strikers, an irate Truman asked Congress for the authority to draft the striking miners. Word came that the strike had been settled while Truman was addressing Congress, but the incident left many union members and liberal Democrats convinced that the new president was anti-labor, an impression which Truman would have to fight mightily to change before the

1948 election. Truman's reaction in fact said more about his sensitivity to what he perceived as personal slights by overbearing labor leaders than a hostility to workers themselves or even unions in general, but that distinction was difficult to discern at the time.

THE POLITICS OF INFLATION

The troubles with labor were made more acute by the general problem of inflation. Contrary to early fears of rampant unemployment, that was not the problem – inflation was. The pressure on prices which had marked the war years, despite government controls, threatened to grow with the coming of peace. Increased take-home pay led to more money in family bank accounts, but during the war there were few consumer items to buy. Productive capacity was dedicated first to war goods. The result was forced savings, which when combined with the suppressed demand of the depression years, left the American people eager and able to spend when the war ended. With few goods immediately available, however, the result was inflation.

Wartime controls by the National War Labor Board were kept in place initially despite the end of hostilities. Fearing a burst of inflation, Truman established the Office of Economic Stabilization in February 1946, and asked Congress for authority to continue price controls. In response, Congress produced an amended, weak bill extending Truman's powers. Price controls abruptly ended on 30 June, when Truman vetoed the bill, apparently believing that it was so weak that it was worse than no bill at all. A burst of inflation followed, causing Truman to reverse himself and ask for another bill, which was revived in modified form on 25 July. Then, in October, Truman opted for de-control of prices, resulting in a 10 percent inflation rate in 1946. The near-universal view was that Truman's handling of the situation had been inept, and it contributed to a growing sense that the man from Missouri was simply not up to the job.

Inflation also contributed to the growing political conservatism that was increasingly evident during the war. New Deal liberalism* was possible in large part because of the economic calamity of the Great Depression. Private institutions, whether businesses or charities, proved incapable of handling the emergency, and Americans overcame their traditional aversion to a large federal government. Inflation reversed that dynamic. Since the federal government was supposed to control prices, it was blamed for inflation. Conservatives used inflation to highlight the problems of government intervention in the economy, leading to a general rebellion against government controls and regulation.

Whatever their political meaning, the economic troubles of the early Truman years actually masked the fundamental strength of the American economy. Labor strife and inflation were merely short-term pains of reconversion. In reality, the United States was in sound economic shape. The fiscal policies of the war years had revived the American economy, while taxes and the demand for labor helped equalize the distribution of national income. In short, more people had more money to spend. The redistribution of income downward during the war (the only time this happened in the twentieth century) reversed the economic dilemma of the 1920s. Now there were plenty of customers waiting to buy consumer products, and it simply took time for industry to be able to produce them. Once business reconverted to civilian purposes, the economy took off. More people climbed into the middle class and productivity increased.

Government played a part as well. Wartime savings combined with the GI Bill* to create dramatic economic growth. The GI Bill, passed toward the end of the war, subsidized the housing, education, training, and businesses of millions of returning veterans. Between 1946 and 1956, 7.8 million veterans took advantage of the GI Bill, and by taking many men out of the labor pool and putting them in college, it helped to make smooth the transition to a peacetime economy. Government housing and business loans given to the veterans helped create jobs in the economy. The federal government spent $3.7 billion on GI Bill benefits between 1945 and 1949. As such, it constituted the only large, new domestic spending project of the Truman years. While liberal proposals fared poorly with Congress in general, the GI Bill was sold as an expression of gratitude to American veterans, not as a new entitlement program (though liberals certainly hoped it would establish a precedent which could later be extended to all Americans). The resulting boom in the postwar economy set the pattern for American life over the next 20 years: the growth of suburbs (also aided by the mass production techniques applied to the housing industry in places like Levittown*), the consumer culture, increased recreation and leisure, and the affluent one-income nuclear family, where mothers could afford to stay home with their children.

None of these major areas of tremendous social change are reflected in the politics of the age. In part because of the unusual degree of upheaval in recent years, the political arena produced a period of political conservatism focused on preservation of the *status quo* and not responsive to the dramatically changing nature of American life. The return of prosperity in particular gave Americans a feeling of complacency, a sense that America's major political and economic problems had been solved. With the scarcity of the depression behind them, and New Deal reforms in place to guard against a repetition of that economic calamity, the public was not in the mood for still more political change. This complacency, reinforced by the growing red scare* at home and abroad, masked underlying changes which would later rend American society in the 1960s.

CHAPTER FIVE

CONSERVATIVE RESURGENCE

Liberals had hoped it would be otherwise. They had looked on with dismay when FDR said that Dr. New Deal had given way to Dr. Win-the-War. But FDR had assured them that the return of peace would bring a return of liberal reform. Their hero's death had left many unsure about the future. Harry Truman sought to revive the New Deal in his first address to Congress after the surrender of Japan, with an ambitious 21-point program, but met an entirely unreceptive Congress [*Doc. 3*]. In the end, his presidency became one of defending, not expanding, the New Deal.

Truman had a brief honeymoon with the public: his approval rating stood at 87 percent in June 1945, and was still at 82 percent in October. These unusually high numbers are largely due to transitory factors: the initial reflex of the public to rally around the new president and the successful completion of the war. Truman was unable to translate that good will into concrete political support for his domestic agenda, however. He spent most of his presidency defensively battling Congress, holding the line against attacks on the New Deal. The fundamentally negative character of Truman's presidency on the domestic front is best illustrated by his veto record. In his nearly eight years as president, Truman vetoed 250 acts of Congress (12 of which were overridden). This total was the most since Andrew Johnson, another 'accidental' president who assumed the presidency after the death of a beloved wartime leader.

THE DILEMMA OF LIBERALISM

As was the case with his foreign policy, Truman's early domestic record was marked by a certain ambivalence. Truman was pulled in different directions. On the one hand, Truman was a reliable New Deal liberal who consistently supported FDR in Congress during the 1930s and 1940s. Like most liberals of the era, he believed that government had a positive role to play in improving the lives of ordinary people. (In 1944, the liberal opinion journal, *The New Republic*, gave him a 98 percent liberal rating.) But Harry Truman was also a good Democrat, and it is important to keep in mind that not all Democrats were liberals. The New Deal coalition that Roosevelt constructed in the 1930s was an inherently unstable one, made up of labor, urban liberals, southern and midwestern rural Democrats, and ethnic and racial minorities. Southern Democrats in particular often opposed the liberalism of the other factions in the party. The Democrats had been held together in part by Roosevelt's charismatic leadership, particularly his uncanny ability to make all parties to a conflict believe that he really agreed with them.

Truman lacked that ability. In many ways, Harry Truman was more a reflection of his party than a leader of it. Truman possessed a native personal conservatism that made him suspicious of those he derisively called the 'professional liberals.' His midwest populism distrusted the elite northeastern liberalism of some of FDR's associates. He was out of the Populist-Progressive tradition, with a reflexive bias against not only Wall Street and big business, but elites of all kinds. He was also a practical politician, as seen by his relationship with his political patron, Kansas City political machine boss Tom Pendergast. While scrupulously guarding his personal integrity, Truman was not above making the compromises and back-room deals which are necessary in politics, a trait which often outraged more purely idealistic liberals.

Truman's appeal to both the liberal and conservative wings of the Democratic Party was the key reason he was chosen as vice-president in 1944. Sensing the conservative drift of American politics during the war, the party bosses refused to countenance the renomination of the incumbent, Henry Wallace, and insisted on a candidate who was more reliable and less liberal. In Truman, they found their man. During his years as president, Truman would oversee the transformation of the Democratic Party from the New Deal liberalism of the 1930s to the cold war liberalism* of the postwar era. The former saw the need for widespread reform and change, with a large role for government to play in regulating the American economy, while the latter accepted the fundamental soundness of the American political and economic system, and saw the greatest challenges to the United States not at home but abroad [61].

Truman's liberal streak is evident in the 21-point program he presented to Congress in September 1945 [Doc. 3]. The liberal laundry list was an ambitious attempt to resurrect the New Deal. Echoing FDR's 1944 address calling for an 'economic bill of rights,' Truman came out for full employment, expanded unemployment compensation, housing legislation, hospital construction, farm price supports, small business assistance, public works, national health insurance, aid to education, and expansion of Social Security. In the words of one Republican, 'It is just a case of out-New Dealing the New Deal' [64 p. 50]. Truman made a clear statement that he was a liberal and would pursue FDR's reform agenda.

Although Truman certainly talked a good game, many liberals were suspicious of him, if only because he had replaced the heir apparent Wallace and had thus proven himself more acceptable to conservatives. Liberal critics pointed out that of 125 federal openings, Truman appointed 49 bankers, financiers and industrialists, 31 career military men, and 17 business lawyers [138 *p. 46*]. They neglected to point out that FDR had appointed his share of businessmen to federal jobs too, but liberals could always tell themselves that that was due to the war emergency or political necessity, not free choice. The 'real' Roosevelt, they believed, was the one who denounced the 'economic royalists' in the mid-1930s. Truman seemed to keep company with such people out of choice, not necessity. One by one, the liberals Truman inherited from FDR left the new administration: Treasury Secretary Henry Morgenthau, Interior Secretary Harold Ickes, and lastly Wallace himself, whom FDR had made Commerce Secretary as a consolation prize for having lost the vice-presidency to Truman.

Liberals were also dismayed by Truman's failure to get results. His program's reception in Congress was less than enthusiastic, and Truman received the blame. In reality, there was no constituency in Congress for the widespread reform Truman advocated. Although there were nominally Democratic majorities in both Houses, Congress had been dominated since 1938 by a coalition of Republicans and conservative Southern Democrats, and was not interested in reforms now that the crisis of the Depression was only a memory. Symbolic of its aversion to substantive change, Congress did pass a watered-down Full Employment Act*, which called for the less demanding goal of 'maximum' rather than 'full' employment, making it clear that despite the original intention of the legislation, employment would not be the sole concern of economic policy. Instead of guaranteeing health insurance, Congress approved a Hospital Construction Act which benefited builders and contractors. Congress also signaled a reversal on civil rights and eliminated the Fair Employment Practices Commission (FEPC)* [30].

Liberals blamed Truman for these setbacks, ignoring FDR's inability to work his will on Congress after 1938. Many New Deal programs were gutted or eliminated during the war as prosperity returned and the national mood turned more conservative. Liberals assumed that when the war ended, they could resume the economic and social reform of the New Deal, and FDR's rhetoric toward the end of the war indicated that he had similar hopes. When that revival failed to materialize, they blamed Truman, rather than the generally conservative trend of American politics.

What liberals failed to see was the extent to which the very success of some New Deal reforms had undermined the appeal of further reforms. Regulation of the stock market, federal deposit insurance, unemployment insurance, and old age pensions had taken much of the terror out of the vicissitudes of the economy for most middle-class Americans. The New Deal created a degree of 'social security' hitherto unknown in American history which sapped support for reform. In short, New Deal liberals had expectations that were bound to be disappointed. In the political climate of 1945–46, neither Roosevelt nor Wallace could have produced the enthusiasm for reform necessary to bring about significant change. New Deal liberalism was not in tune with the general public, and Truman made a convenient scapegoat for the failure of the New Deal to return to the political heights it briefly reached in the mid-1930s.

In their disappointment, New Dealers missed the greater significance of the political events of 1945–46. While the Full Employment Act which eventually passed Congress seemed to them an empty statement of benign intention, it was also an official acceptance of the concept that government had an obligation to manage the economy, a controversial idea not too many years before [*Doc. 4*]. Admittedly, Truman was not another FDR, nor was he even a Henry Wallace. On the other hand, he also was not a Herbert Hoover, or as Democrats would realize in 1948, a Thomas Dewey. The New Deal had achieved major changes in the way that the public viewed the role of government, but further reform would have to wait until a later, less conservative day, when the holes in the social safety net of the New Deal would come into harsher relief. In the near term, however, the overwhelming reality of American politics was the drift away from New Deal-style policies.

'HAD ENOUGH?'

Truman's seemingly inept, contradictory and confused handling of postwar issues dovetailed nicely with Republican plans for the 1946 campaign. The Democratic Party had been in power for nearly 14 years. The watershed 1932 election gave the Democrats complete control of both the legislative and executive branches of government, which they had held ever since. As the Congressional elections of 1946 approached, it became clear that the public was growing tired of this uninterrupted winning streak. Republicans, sensing the chance to escape from under the cloud of Herbert Hoover and the Depression, expertly capitalized on the prevailing mood. Their simple campaign slogan, 'Had Enough?' was brilliantly designed to mean all things to all people. It captured both short-term frustration with Truman, and a longer-term sense that the Democrats had held the reins of power for too long. For those unhappy with foreign affairs, it meant 'had enough appeasement?' For those alarmed by rising prices, it meant 'had enough inflation?' For those opposed to big government liberalism, it meant 'had enough bureaucracy?' Without explicitly focusing on what they would do differently, Republicans effectively seized upon the notion that the time had come for a change.

The slogan also was meant to take advantage of public unhappiness with Harry Truman. In the weeks and months after FDR's death, most Americans were willing to give the relatively unknown Truman a chance. With the passage of time, however, he was becoming increasingly unpopular (his approval rating was only 34 percent in July 1946). To liberals, he was an unacceptable heir to FDR's legacy. To mainstream Democrats, he was an ineffective party leader. To conservatives, he was more of the same New Deal liberalism they had always opposed. To many nonideological voters, he was simply not up to the job. He was too ordinary, he was not the leader FDR had been. His own ambivalence about where he wanted to take the country may have reflected the views of the American people, but he also became the scapegoat for their own indecisiveness. Rather than mirror back on them their uncertainty, Americans were looking for a leader in a time of great change. To the majority of voters in November 1946, Harry Truman was not that leader.

The result was an electoral disaster for the Democrats. When the counting was done, Republicans had won majorities in both Houses of Congress for the first time since the Depression began. Their margin was 245–188 in the House, and 51–45 in the Senate. Moreover, the 1946 elections were a débâcle not only for the Democrats, but specifically for liberals: many of the most liberal members of Congress were defeated in their bids for re-election. Liberals were dispirited: FDR was gone, and his successor had led them to political disaster. Wallace and Ickes, the last remnants of the Roosevelt administration, had left the cabinet. In foreign policy, the drift was toward confrontation with the Soviets. Conservatives were ascendant in Congress and might soon regain the presidency.

In contrast, Republicans gleefully took their victory in 1946 as a sign that their long absence from the White House would soon end as well. Without Franklin Roosevelt on the ticket, Democrats stood little chance of winning the presidency in 1948, especially if the inept Truman should be foolish enough to run for election in his own right. With control of Congress, they could reverse the dangerous drift toward socialism of the New Deal, they could use their control of committees to expose communist agents who slipped into government under the protection of New Dealers.

Both liberals and conservatives underestimated Harry Truman. Without a doubt, Truman's first 18 months as president were marked by uncertainty as he grappled with the tremendous changes in the country as well as the incredible burdens he faced upon suddenly assuming the presidency. With each passing day he became more comfortable with his powers and responsibilities, and his personal insecurities diminished. Counted out by both sides of the political spectrum, Truman felt liberated to be his own man, to claim the political center as his own. If he were to go down, he would go down fighting; and if he fought well enough, he would not go down at all.

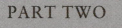

PART TWO   RETRENCHMENT AND
VINDICATION, 1947–48

CHAPTER SIX

THE BIPARTISAN MOMENT IN FOREIGN POLICY

The Republican victory in the 1946 Congressional elections led the Truman administration to change its strategy on both domestic and foreign policy. Republican hostility to liberalism caused Truman to adopt a confrontational policy toward Congress, defending the New Deal against attacks and blaming Congress for failing to act on his reform agenda. In foreign policy, however, Truman could not afford to be confrontational with the Republicans. His evolving policy toward the Soviet Union and the fate of postwar Europe required that he woo the opposition for its support. He sought to revive the wartime sentiment that party politics should stop at the water's edge. He was, for a time, remarkably successful. The bipartisan moment created the foundations of US cold war policy for the next 40 years. At the same time, Truman rallied politically and won the presidency in his own right. The price he paid for that brief consensus and electoral victory was dear, however. The rhetoric he employed and the compromises he made would haunt him for the rest of his years as president.

The bipartisan consensus behind the containment policy of the Truman administration is a major theme of the early cold war. It is important to remember that bipartisanship was in fact rather short-lived. The personification of the bipartisan (or even nonpartisan) foreign policy was Truman's new Secretary of State, former General George C. Marshall, who replaced the more political James F. Byrnes. As the leader of the American military during World War II, Marshall was an inspired choice to forge a bipartisan foreign policy. His patriotism and ability were seemingly beyond reproach [111; 125]. (Nonetheless, within four years, Joseph McCarthy would accuse Marshall of being part of a communist conspiracy. There could be no better symbol of the fleeting nature of the bipartisan moment.)

It is also worth noting that the bipartisan consensus came only when Truman clearly abandoned his efforts to maintain a normal working relationship with the Soviet Union. Truman's embrace of a policy of ongoing confrontation with the Soviets forged an alliance between internationalist and anti-communist Democrats and Republicans. This centrist coalition also marginalized both isolationist Republicans and left-liberal Democrats and thereby achieved a measure of bipartisan (though by no means unanimous) support for Truman's foreign policy. It would not last.

CONTAINMENT: THE TRUMAN DOCTRINE

The decisive moment for the Truman administration came in early 1947. Several events coincided to make it abundantly clear that the United States had some basic decisions to make about the future direction of its foreign policy. The Soviet Union had largely consolidated its control over eastern Europe through communist puppet regimes. In western Europe, the residual effects of the war were threatening to change the political and economic climate. On the continent, the physical devastation of the war and its economic consequences made socialist and even communist parties more attractive to desperate voters. In such important nations as France and Italy, communist parties might come to power democratically if drastic steps were not taken. Simultaneously, Great Britain was becoming increasingly unable to carry its imperial burdens in the postwar era. Its colonies were chafing under British rule, and economically, the government was practically broke. To the United States, this meant that Britain was no longer an equal partner; the British were dependent on the United States, economically and militarily [69].

The common element connecting these developments was the prospect of a vacuum of power in Europe, one which American policy-makers assumed would be filled by the Soviet Union if the United States did not act first. When faced with this stark choice, the administration took action. Truman's rather *ad hoc* and ambivalent foreign policy was no longer a viable option. Either the United States had to commit itself unequivocally to the emerging policy of containment, or abandon it and accept the possible consequences, including a Europe increasingly under Soviet sway.

Since the time Truman became president, he had been moving, however haltingly, in the direction of what came to be called containment. The policy received its first clear statement in State Department official George Kennan's 'Long Telegram,' in February 1946 [*Doc. 5*]. The policy tacitly accepted Soviet dominance as a *fait accompli* in eastern Europe, but was determined to prevent any further Soviet gains. It reflected the view that American and Soviet interests were not compatible, and that Soviet advances constituted American setbacks. If such advances were to proceed without resistance, the Truman administration feared that, in the long run, the world balance of power would shift in favor of the Soviet Union. Europe would be dominated by communist regimes subservient to the Soviet Union. With effective control of the Eurasian land mass, the Soviets could use their enhanced military and economic power to intimidate others, and isolate the United States. Thus isolated, the United States would be forced to hunker down, militarize for the defense of its territory, and impose domestic economic controls to survive in a world hostile to capitalism and free trade. In brief, the world could become an implacably hostile place which threatened the maintenance of American liberty and prosperity [84].

This nightmare scenario betrays the basic insecurity that lay behind postwar American confidence. For all of its history, Americans had seen the rest of the world in far less apocalyptic terms, with more disdain than fear. Occasional threats would arise, the country would gird itself for action, dispatch the enemy, and resume its geopolitical slumber. In the late war, two foreign dragons had been slain: Nazi Germany and Imperial Japan. The American people and their representatives sought to demobilize quickly and return to normal life. The Truman years instead saw a major shift away from this tradition.

In reflecting on why the war came, Truman administration officials concluded that the American retreat from world involvement (symbolized by the Senate's rejection of American membership in the League of Nations after World War I) had been in part responsible. So too had the short-sighted economic policies of the 1920s and 1930s, which produced protectionism and depression. The war had taught two hard lessons: the oceans no longer provided adequate security and the American economy could not prosper alone. These ideas, when combined with the perception of an aggressive Soviet leadership intent on undermining American ideals and interests, created an historic shift in attitude. Henceforth, American peace and prosperity could only be guaranteed by an active, assertive, and continuous policy of world leadership.

The moment of truth which crystallized these issues for the administration came with the British notification on 24 February 1947 that it would no longer be able to carry the load in propping up the anti-communist regime in Greece under challenge by a communist insurgency. Greece had been a traditional area of British influence, but the new reality was that Britain could not afford to maintain its position there. With the insurgents receiving aid from the neighboring communist regime of Marshal Tito in Yugoslavia, there was a growing danger of a communist triumph in Greece. If the United States did not step in, the British warned, the Soviets inevitably would [68].

Britain's admission of its inability to carry its load represented a role reversal and passing of the torch of leadership. Many times in the past, the United States had crafted its foreign policies to hitchhike on Britain's power. The Monroe Doctrine* of 1823 relied ultimately on the fact that American and British interests in Latin America coincided, and the United States could count on the British Navy to enforce the American policy of opposition to new colonization in the western hemisphere. In the 1840s, Americans followed Britain's forceful entry into the China market. The American Open Door policy* of free trade with China at the turn of the century similarly depended on its coinciding with the British view. As late as the 1930s, Americans largely deferred to British leadership regarding European policy. The war had completed the long historical process by which the former colony replaced its mother country as a world power. It was not, as Henry Wallace and his followers feared, a case of the United States defending British imperial interests, as much as it was the United States making those interests its own.

The British had long sought to thwart Russian ambitions of access to the Mediterranean Sea. Greece and Turkey thus represented barrier states: as long as they were aligned with the west, Russia would be stymied. By early 1947, both nations were under Soviet pressure. In 1946, the Soviets had sought to use their commanding presence on Turkey's border to convince the Turkish government to grant the Soviet Union joint control of the straits between the Black Sea and the Mediterranean. Truman forcefully supported Turkish resistance. In Greece, communist insurgents threatened to topple the anti-communist government, in which case (it was assumed) the new communist government would grant the Soviets access to Greek ports.

The Truman administration decided (1) that American assistance to both nations was essential, and (2) to use the crisis to make the broader case for an internationalist foreign policy of containment. The rationale behind the change had been coalescing for months. All that was needed was an event to provide the proper context for its direct, clear and public expression. Truman knew that the Republican-controlled Congress was not likely to be enthusiastic about a $400 million foreign aid proposal ($250 million for Greece, $150 million for Turkey). Some Republicans remained isolationist in their foreign policy, and many more were committed to reducing government spending. Truman had to make the case for Greece and Turkey not on its merits alone, but by placing it into a larger context. As Secretary Marshall put it in a private meeting with Congressional leaders, failure to meet this crisis might result ultimately in 'Soviet domination [of] Europe, the Middle East and Asia' [54 *p. 391*].

While Republican internationalists like Senator Arthur Vandenberg, chairman of the Senate Foreign Relations Committee, were rather easily convinced, others in Congress and the public needed more. As Vandenberg put it, Truman needed to scare the hell out of the American people. Only by framing the issue in stark terms could Truman hope to convince Americans to support him. For what Truman was actually calling for was not simply aid to Greece and Turkey, but a peacetime reversal of the American foreign policy tradition of isolationism.

Thus when Truman addressed Congress on 12 March 1947, he said that the problem of Greece and Turkey represented only '[o]ne aspect of the present situation,' which had 'broad implications' [*Doc. 8*]. American security was undermined and threatened whenever a totalitarian regime was imposed on a nation, Truman argued. Thus, he concluded: 'it must be the policy of the United States to support free peoples who are resisting attempted subjugation by armed minorities or by outside pressures.' His policy, he said, was a continuation of what the United States fought for in World War II: 'the creation of conditions in which we and other nations will be able to work out a way of life free from coercion.' It would be foolish to succumb to the temptation to withdraw from the world. He reminded his audience that his request amounted 'to little more than 1/10 of 1 percent' of what the country had spent on the war. 'It is only common sense,' Truman asserted, 'that we should safeguard this investment and make sure it was not in vain.' Whether Americans liked it or not, world leadership was now their destiny: 'Great responsibilities have been placed upon us by the swift movement of events,' and the peace of the world was at stake [*Doc. 8*]. Despite the surrender of Germany and Japan, the work of World War II was not over. A new phase had begun: the cold war.

Truman was convinced that he had to speak in stark, universal tones to produce the appropriate response from the Congress and the public. He had to impress upon them the seriousness with which he viewed the situation, and thus he invoked the ultimate metaphor, war, and framed the problem in moral terms which Americans could understand and support: freedom versus tyranny. While he diplomatically refrained from directly naming the Soviet Union or communism, Truman's intent was clear. A new enemy to freedom had emerged, and if the sacrifices of the war were not to be in vain, then the United States would have to assume the burden of defending freedom in times of peace as it had in time of war.

Truman's tactics made short-term political sense, but carried with them dangerous potential. By universalizing this particular crisis, Truman failed to distinguish between vital and peripheral interests. He stated forthrightly that 'totalitarian regimes imposed upon free peoples ... undermine the foundations of international peace and hence the security of the United States' [*Doc. 8*]. Having stated the conflict in such stark moral terms, both Truman and his successors would have difficulty explaining why *some* totalitarian regimes did not threaten peace and security. For Truman, China would later present this problem; for his successors, it would be Vietnam. By raising the specter of communist aggression via internal subversion, he also inadvertently added to growing fears of the enemy within which would also come back to haunt him. In the short run, Truman succeeded. Congress approved his request by large majorities. The United States now clearly stood behind the Turkish and Greek regimes, drawing a containment line which the Soviets could not cross.

THE MARSHALL PLAN

While a hard line and financial aid might stiffen the resistance to communist pressures in those nations, a different danger loomed in western Europe. American allies were in desperate economic shape after the war, and recovery was coming slowly if at all. In response, native communist parties were growing in popularity. Many of them had been active in resisting the Nazi occupation and had legitimate nationalist credentials with their peoples. If things did not improve quickly and dramatically, American officials feared, communists might come to power not by aggression or subversion but by democratic election. The $400 million for Greece and Turkey was a mere band-aid when compared to what was necessary for the economic recovery of the rest of Europe, however. Even as the Congress was considering this modest request, the administration turned its attention to a much more ambitious project, a massive economic assistance program which would be known as the Marshall Plan* [50; 62].

The European Recovery Program (ERP) was related to, yet distinct from, the Truman Doctrine. While the program received added urgency from the perception of a communist threat, its origins had much to do with the economic lessons American leaders took from their recent history. Peace was preserved, they believed, not only by firm resistance to aggression, but also by free trade, which gave all nations access to the goods they needed to prosper. Trade eliminated the incentive to seize territory in order to attain access to raw materials and markets, it created prosperous peoples who would support democracy and resist the temptations of totalitarian solutions to economic deprivation. Thus it was in the interest of the United States that the nations of western Europe, devastated by war, get back on their feet economically. The alternative was a nightmare. Scarcity would lead to protectionism, the opposite of free trade. Should such protectionism become dominant, it would deprive the American economy of the trade partners it needed to thrive, with inevitably adverse effects on the American standard of living.

Even if the Soviet Union did not exist, the Truman administration would have needed the Marshall Plan to secure American economic security. Austerity programs in western Europe would limit American imports, thus cutting off markets essential to American businesses. The Marshall Plan thus tied American economic assistance to the purchase of American goods. The existence (and hostility) of the Soviet Union was of immeasurable benefit to the argument for the program. If capitalism and democracy failed to produce prosperity in Europe, the administration argued, more radical ideologies like communism might gain adherents. A plan of economic aid to Europe therefore had the dual benefits of diminishing the potential electoral appeal of communism and restoring the economic health of America's most important trading partners.

By April 1947, Secretary of State Marshall was convinced that a substantial American aid program for Europe was essential, and he had State Department officials develop a plan. In a commencement address at Harvard in June, Marshall invited the nations of Europe to approach the United States with their suggestions for a comprehensive, multinational plan for economic recovery. America's western European allies responded enthusiastically, while the Soviets reacted suspiciously. Despite the recent announcement of the Truman Doctrine, the Soviets and their client states had not been excluded from the invitation. American officials did not expect them to reply favorably, since any plan acceptable to the United States would require aid recipients to open their economies to American trade. The Soviets saw this as an attempt to undermine their economic system, by exposing it to the corrupting influence of capitalism. Predictably, Stalin refused and ordered the satellites to do likewise. Another step in the division of Europe had been taken.

Believing that the Truman Doctrine and the Marshall Plan represented a clear policy of confrontation with the Soviet Union, Stalin tightened his grip on the governments of eastern Europe. The key event was the *coup d'état* in Czechoslovakia in February 1948. Since the end of the war, the Czechs had managed to maintain a semblance of democracy and independence unique in eastern Europe. The seizure of power by Czech communists and the death of Foreign Minister Jan Masaryk (allegedly a suicide, but under the circumstances, many observers suspected foul play) led to a 'war scare' in March that helped remove remaining objections to the Marshall Plan [79]. The administration had a relatively easy time in Congress. While some Republicans, like Senator Robert Taft, were opposed to the high cost of the Marshall Plan, internationalist Republicans led by Senator Vandenberg supported the program. Soviet rejection of the plan (and their increasingly heavy hand in their satellites) helped convince many congressmen to support it. The combination of fear of communism and economic self-interest prevailed, with both Houses of Congress approving the plan in April 1948.

The cost of the Marshall Plan was a major issue. The initial appropriation in June 1948 was for $5 billion, approximately 12 percent of the federal budget. Truman was determined to get Congressional approval without having to raise taxes, which might provoke a negative reaction from the public. It was difficult enough to get the public to accept massive foreign aid; raising their taxes to do it might well kill the program (and would not be particularly good politics in an election year). The only way Truman could devote the resources necessary to the Marshall Plan was to restrain defense spending, which he did. He kept the Pentagon's budget at $13 billion in 1948, and $13.1 billion in 1949, despite the Defense Department's request for $23 billion. Truman managed to restrain defense spending and get economic assistance for western Europe, but once again not without cost. When the cold war took a turn for the worse in 1949, Truman would come under severe criticism for his fiscal conservatism at the expense of the defense budget.

However necessary the policies adopted by the Truman administration may have seemed, they no doubt intensified the escalating cold war. Both sides moved to consolidate their position in their spheres. With the United States apparently moving to form a western bloc, the Soviets increased their grip on their sphere, as noted above. American success in undermining popular support for communist parties in western Europe (including covert aid to anti-communist political parties in Italy to ensure communist failure in the elections there in 1948) diminished the possibility that Soviet influence would replace American influence outside the existing Soviet sphere in Europe. In response to the Czech coup and warnings that western Europe might be vulnerable to a Soviet offensive, in March 1948 Truman asked for and received Congressional authorization to resume the military draft, raising the possibility that the cold war in Europe might turn hot.

THE BERLIN BLOCKADE AND AIRLIFT

One decision made by the Americans, that a strong western Europe required a revived West Germany, led to the final serious crisis in Europe during the Truman years: the Berlin blockade*. At the end of the war, the victorious allies had divided Germany into four occupation zones, pending a final peace settlement. The deterioration of the alliance meant that three years after Germany's surrender, no agreement had been reached. For reasons made obvious by their recent history, the Soviets feared a united Germany. Twice already in the century, Germany had invaded Russia. The last invasion cost the Soviets dearly, and they had succeeded in defeating it in part due to an alliance with Britain and the United States. A Germany allied with Britain and the United States might achieve a different result. Thus the Soviets viewed with some alarm western moves to consolidate their occupation zones in Germany.

The introduction of a new currency in the western zones on 18 June 1948 provided the occasion for Soviet action. Stalin began the Berlin blockade, cutting off access to the western part of the divided German capital, which lay completely within the Soviet occupation zone. Stalin's motives are as always somewhat opaque, but it seems likely that he was trying to force the western allies to abandon their plans for West Germany, or failing that, force them out of Berlin to facilitate his own consolidation of the Soviet zone. Truman refused to do either. He quickly decided: 'We'll stay in Berlin – come what may' [54 *p. 444*]. To the president, Stalin's bluster on Berlin was a test of containment. If the Soviets succeeded in bullying the west out of Berlin, it would undermine confidence in American policy in Europe. Firm resolve, Kennan had argued in the Long Telegram, would force the Soviets to back down.

The question was 'how?' The United States could have insisted upon its rights of access to West Berlin and directly challenged the blockade on the land by trying to force its way in. Such a confrontation threatened to escalate into conflict between US and Soviet forces, with the potential for starting World War III. Not wishing to ignite a war (particularly when American actions might be seen as provocative in the eyes of the rest of the world), Truman demurred. The only alternative remaining was to supply Berlin by air. This option had the additional advantage of placing the onus for any hostilities squarely on the Soviets. If they chose to shoot down planes bringing food to hungry people, the world would know who wanted war. To impress Stalin with the potential consequences of armed conflict, Truman rather publicly sent three squadrons of B-29 bombers to Britain: planes which might be – but were not – carrying atomic bombs [117; 154].

Thus began the Berlin airlift. Initially seen as a stopgap measure, it soon evolved into an around-the-clock operation which went on for nearly a year. At its height in 1949, a plane was landing on one of two Berlin airfields every 90 seconds. After long and drawn out negotiations, in which it became clear that the west would not budge, the Soviets finally lifted the blockade in May 1949 without accomplishing either of their objectives. The creation of an independent West Germany proceeded, countered by East Germany in the Soviet sector. More significantly, Soviet truculence over Berlin had helped consolidate anti-Soviet opinion in both western Europe and the United States.

Although Berlin would remain a source of tension throughout the cold war (particularly in 1961, when the East German regime constructed the Berlin Wall to prevent East Germans from defecting to the west), in retrospect it is clear that the Berlin blockade and airlift signaled the stabilization of the cold war in Europe. Had either side truly desired war to alter the *status quo* in Europe, the Berlin crisis presented the opportunity. The caution exercised by both sides indicated their tacit acceptance of the division of Europe into American and Soviet spheres. American and Soviet vital interests were now well-defined, and neither would challenge seriously the position of the other in Europe for the remainder of the cold war. The western powers remained in West Berlin facing their eastern counterparts at Checkpoint Charlie. They would still be there 40 years later when the communist regime in East Germany disintegrated at the end of the cold war.

CHAPTER SEVEN

THE NATIONAL SECURITY STATE AND THE RED SCARE

Nine days after Truman addressed Congress on Greece and Turkey, he introduced a loyalty program for federal employees. The proximity of the two events captures the close connection between the burgeoning cold war and the emergence of what some historians have called the 'national security state*.' As the threat from abroad seemed to increase, the Truman administration took ever greater steps toward increasing American security by both revamping the bureaucracy of national defense and by taking steps to root out suspected spies in government [45; 150].

THE NATIONAL SECURITY ACT

The National Security Act of 1947 (NSA)*, passed by Congress in July of that year, was both an immediate response to short-term problems and part of a larger trend in the expansion of the power of the president. In the short-term, recent events of the war and immediate postwar period made a strong case for a reorganization of the military and intelligence establishment. The country had been woefully unprepared for World War II. Inter-service rivalries and the lack of an intelligence network were particularly severe problems that had hampered American performance. As the Truman administration moved toward the conclusion that the United States must remain permanently active in world affairs, the conviction grew that reorganization was essential to the smooth implementation of American policies [150].

Although the nation had always been concerned with its security, the term 'national security,' which became prominent in the 1940s, meant the inter-relatedness of political, military and economic factors. As American leaders came to appreciate the ways in which various US interests were linked, it became necessary to have the means for coordinating the policies which affected the national security. The National Security Act is thus the legislative manifestation of the realization of the complex global interests of the United States in the Truman years. The more *ad hoc*, inefficient formation of policy which sufficed for all of American history had become an unaffordable luxury for a superpower.

The improved organization promised by the National Security Act appealed to Truman's personal desire for clarity and efficiency, which went back to his earliest political experiences in politics back in Missouri and continued in his wartime investigations of waste and fraud in defense industries. Rather than two separate cabinet officers heading the War and Navy Departments, for example, there would be a single Secretary of Defense at the head of the National Military Establishment. (The replacement of the title 'Secretary of War' with 'Secretary of Defense' captured the post-Pearl Harbor focus on preparedness rather than reaction, the prevention rather than the fighting of wars.) The new National Security Council (NSC)* would bring together the president, vice-president, secretaries of state and defense and others to coordinate national security policy. As an advisory body, it was meant to create consensus policies which reflected the president's views.

The NSA had another component which reflected a growing maturity in the American view of the modern world. It created the Central Intelligence Agency (CIA)*. Prior to World War II, there had been no comparable US organization. Intelligence gathering had been a function of the State Department and American embassies. During the war, the Office of Strategic Services (OSS) organized American intelligence operations and carried out covert actions. Such activities were seen by some Americans as a wartime expedience, but the cold war soon convinced Truman that a permanent intelligence operation was essential to avoiding another surprise like Pearl Harbor. The old-world attitude that gentlemen do not read each other's mail (expressed by FDR's and Truman's Secretary of War, Henry Stimson), was no longer sustainable. A shrinking and dangerous world required espionage, even covert action. In the CIA, the United States created a vehicle for an expansion of executive power, largely beyond true oversight by the legislative branch (Congress routinely approved CIA funding without really knowing exactly what the agency was doing with it). Over the years, especially in the Eisenhower and Kennedy administrations, covert actions by the CIA would become an increasingly integral part of American foreign policy. Under Truman, however, its primary function remained intelligence gathering.

THE ENEMY WITHIN

American naiveté about the world of diplomacy and espionage is an important factor in understanding how the national security state affected domestic politics in the United States. The American people, and to a certain extent their representatives, wanted to return to what the previous generation had called 'normalcy' after the war. The most graphic illustration of that desire was the rapid demobilization of American forces after the war: from 12 million in uniform and a $90.9 billion defense budget in June 1945 to 1.7 million and $10.3 billion in June 1947, with most of those soldiers committed to occupation duties. Americans had been dragged into the war reluctantly (it took the direct, devastating attack on Pearl Harbor to overcome isolationism*), and they sought to flee from it enthusiastically. As John Quincy Adams observed in the 1820s, the United States 'goes not abroad in search of monsters to destroy.' When the monsters came to her, the United States like any nation would, sought to destroy them. But Americans also naively believed that, having slain those monsters, they had solved their (and in this case, the world's) problems.

The cold war belied that belief. No sooner had Nazi Germany and Imperial Japan been defeated than a new menace emerged. The Soviet Union combined the only remaining military force capable of threatening American security with an ideology that was hostile to the American political and economic system. To make matters worse, this new enemy had until quite recently been an ally. That new reality required a significant shift in outlook on the part of some Americans, while reinforcing long-standing suspicions on the part of others. For all, the hope that true world peace would follow this most horrible of world wars was shattered.

The resulting disillusionment often took the form of a search for scapegoats. For the Truman administration, the answer was simple: the Soviet Union, not content to co-operate with the United States and the rest of the United Nations, had sought to take advantage of the power vacuum in Europe after the war. Their aggressive, expansionist policies required a firm response and continuing vigilance from the United States. For others, the answer was also simple, but different: the enemy within had helped the Soviets to take advantage of the United States. Soviet gains were not the natural outcome of the conditions on the ground in Europe, but rather the result of subversion. Soviet agents, communists in America, had shaped American policy and advanced the Soviet cause.

American isolationism had always taken part of its inspiration from American fears of being duped by duplicitous foreigners. Washington's farewell address, which gave the nation its admonition against 'entangling alliances,' also warned of another danger. 'Against the insidious wiles of foreign influence,' the retiring president wrote in 1796, 'the jealousy of a free people ought to be *constantly* awake, since history and experience prove that foreign influence is one of the most baneful foes of republican government.' Favoritism toward any nation was dangerous, Washington argued, because it would allow foreigners to take advantage of and work through American political parties. Having insinuated themselves into the American political system, foreign agents would use their American 'dupes and tools' to convince 'the people to surrender their interests.'

To Americans seeking an explanation for the failure of the war to solve their problems in the outside world, Washington's words offered one: the Soviet Union, working through New Deal Democrats, had infiltrated the American government. It had taken advantage of wartime American favoritism toward 'our gallant Soviet allies' to influence American policy in ways that would redound to the postwar advantage of the Soviet Union. The real danger was not in Europe or even in Asia, it was at home. This line of thought was particularly attractive to more isolationist Republicans, like Senator Robert Taft, who sought to reconcile their aversion to a continuing American presence in Europe with their anti-communism. Taft argued that the United States 'should meet communism first here in the United States, bring it out into the open and eliminate its influence' [*Doc. 12*]. The United States had to lead by example, not through an internationalist foreign policy.

If the Truman administration was correct, then the United States could only look forward to years, even decades, of military vigilance, policing Europe indefinitely. If, on the other hand, the real problem lay within, then the solution was not an internationalist foreign policy, but a more aggressive attempt to root out subversives in the American government. That these subversives were also New Dealers only added to the attraction of the theory for Republicans and other conservatives. The republic simultaneously could be made safe from both foreign influence on American diplomacy and left-wing domestic policies, all without abandoning its isolationist tradition.

This point of view was aided immeasurably by the undeniable reality that of course there *was* a Soviet espionage network in the United States. The *Amerasia* case in June 1945* (in which the left-wing magazine was found to possess classified government documents), and the revelation in early 1946 of a Soviet spy ring in Canada focusing on atomic research, alarmed Americans who had thought that their country was immune from such infiltration [76]. The association of espionage with a radical, revolutionary ideology was extremely potent. 'Communism' had long been a catch-all term in the United States, an epithet rather cavalierly hurled at anything strange or unusual. In the midst of labor strife after World War I and the Bolshevik Revolution in Russia, the United States experienced a 'red scare' in which radicals were rounded up, and foreigners deported for their radical politics. Now the 'specter of communism' had returned, this time under the direction of a powerful state and with the assistance of American dupes, 'fellow travelers*,' and 'fifth columnists*.' Anti-communism had the virtue of offering people a simple way to understand a complex world.

That is not to say that anti-communists created a phantom menace, only that they exaggerated the degree of the threat and inaccurately attributed adverse conditions in eastern Europe to communist perfidy in the United States rather than to complex diplomatic and military realities. There was indeed Soviet espionage in the United States, much of it coordinated by the

Communist Party of the United States (CPUS). The recent declassification of the Venona Project, a long-standing American effort to decrypt Soviet intelligence messages, has revealed the extent of Soviet penetration of the American government during the 1930s and 1940s. This intelligence material, in combination with limited access to KGB files, has confirmed that both Alger Hiss and Julius Rosenberg, who were at the center of the two most famous espionage cases of the Truman years, were in fact working for Soviet intelligence.

While these revelations might be seen as justifying the anti-communist paranoia of the times, the evidence which has emerged also makes clear that American counterintelligence, aided by defections from Soviet ranks, had largely neutralized the Soviet espionage ring by late 1945, before the postwar red scare even began [158]. Whatever threat Soviet espionage might have presented during the late 1930s and the war years no longer existed. The red scare itself went beyond a legitimate desire to catch spies. Not only communists but leftists of all kinds became targets as well [140].

The American Communist Party was formed in 1919, and was a member of the Communist International, or Comintern. The party received financial assistance from Moscow and slavishly followed the party line, but it was never a significant factor in American politics. In 1929, it had only 7,000 members. Membership grew in the 1930s due to the Great Depression, when many people came to the conclusion that capitalism did not work. Most people who joined the party soon left it, repulsed by the strict conformity of the party line. Others never actually belonged to the party, but did join small organizations known as front groups and became known as 'fellow travelers.'

Following Moscow's lead, the party abruptly abandoned its anti-fascist stand in 1939 when the Nazi–Soviet non-aggression pact was signed. The shift hurt the party, but Germany's attack on the Soviet Union in 1941 allowed American communists once again to make common cause with other left-liberal groups in the United States, a strategy known as the Popular Front. Membership peaked in 1945 (somewhere between 40 and 50 thousand) and declined significantly thereafter, when the party became thoroughly infiltrated by the FBI. It gained some respectability from its support of the New Deal, civil rights, and unionism during the Popular Front period of the 1930s and its anti-fascism during the war, but the CPUS was always viewed with suspicion by most Americans, and was seen by some conservatives as a greater threat than Nazism in the 1930s. In fact, when the House Committee on Un-American Activities (HUAC)* was created in 1938, it devoted much attention to communists rather than Nazis.

Therefore, there was a solid historical foundation for the domestic anti-communism of the Truman years. It arose out of decades of suspicion of communism by Americans, and their more immediate desire to explain how conditions in Europe had deteriorated so far so fast. It was advanced and encouraged by Republican leaders frustrated by many years in the political wilderness, hesitant to embrace an internationalist foreign policy, and trying to prevent liberal reforms which they believed would take the United States further down the road to socialism and economic ruin. The hunt was on for the enemy within.

Truman was always suspicious of the effort to unmask Soviet agents in the US government. The blatantly political motivation of some Republicans convinced him that the whole effort was partisan, not patriotic. That conviction blinded him to the power of the anti-communist argument and the real concerns many Americans had about espionage. Truman gave little credence to such accusations at first, but after the 1946 election débâcle, he decided that the charge of treason in high places had struck a chord with the public and needed to be addressed. On 25 November 1946, he established the Temporary Commission on Employee Loyalty. Truman was likely motivated by a desire to act before the new Republican Congress forced upon him its own plan, over which he might have little control.

The Commission established loyalty review boards to investigate all new federal employees, and charged all federal offices with the responsibility of checking on the loyalty of current employees. The traditional presumption of innocence was abandoned in the name of national security. Employees now had to prove their loyalty (which was never precisely defined). The program led to an enhanced role for the FBI and its director, J. Edgar Hoover, who was an anti-communist from the first red scare. Despite his fears of creating a 'Gestapo,' Truman continued and institutionalized the program in Executive Order 9835*, creating the Federal Employee Loyalty Program* on 21 March 1947. Sympathy with communism was enough to justify dismissal, and the accused was not entitled to know who the accuser was. Reasonable doubt as to one's loyalty, not proof, was sufficient under the official guidelines: 'reasonable grounds exist for the belief that the person involved is disloyal.' The number of employees affected is a matter of some controversy. Estimates vary widely, with some historians claiming that 12,000 resigned as a result, and others arguing that the real number is between 1,000 and 6,000. Between 400 and 1,200 others were dismissed from their jobs [54 p. 428].

Historians also differ on the question of whether Truman was more of a victim or a perpetrator on this matter. Critics focus on the undeniable fact that the red scare contributed to the success of the Truman Doctrine and Marshall Plan and argue that the president deliberately whipped up domestic anti-communism to advance those foreign policy initiatives [45]. Others argue that the president only reluctantly accepted the necessity of a loyalty program, which was forced on him by public and political pressure. His rhetoric, while clearly focusing on the Soviet threat, did not paint that threat as an internal one. Truman even refrained from using the word 'communism' in his address to Congress. Overall, the administration's foreign policy was based on the presumption that it was Soviet power and its potential to make mischief that represented the real threat to American interests, not espionage or domestic communism.

Nonetheless, by conflating the military threat posed by the Soviet state and the ideological threat of the very idea of communism, Truman did contribute to public confusion and helped foster conditions in which the red scare flourished. The Truman administration never clearly delineated the difference to the American people (one could argue the same was true of the United States throughout the cold war). In the Truman Doctrine speech, the president said that the enemy was 'a way of life based upon the will of a minority forcibly imposed upon the majority' [*Doc. 8*]. It was therefore not a state or its military might, but an *idea* which the United States needed to resist. Ideas can cross borders without detection, ideas cannot be fought with guns, as Taft argued [*Doc. 12*]. They must be exposed and discredited. As Truman's own Attorney General Tom Clark put it, the communists 'are everywhere ... and each carries with him the germs of death for society' [138 *p. 75*]. Framing the American cause as a battle of ideas and ideals, Truman was able to husband support for his departure from American foreign policy tradition, but at the cost of inflaming domestic fears that the nameless, faceless enemy might be anywhere.

The red scare took various forms – the Loyalty Program, Congressional investigations, legal actions and even private actions. The Loyalty Program led to the creation of the Attorney General's list, which identified allegedly 'subversive' organizations. Membership in any such group could constitute grounds for dismissal, association with a member was considered suspicious in itself. These investigations, while representing attacks on civil liberties, were at least targeted at government employees. Others, however, did not limit themselves to those in positions to know government secrets or directly influence public policy.

HUAC became active in pursuit of communists in all aspects of American life. As J. Parnell Thomas, the Republican chairman from New Jersey said, the Committee 'has the responsibility of exposing and spotlighting subversive elements wherever they exist' [13 *p. 1*]. In 1947, with Thomas at the helm, the Committee launched an investigation 'to determine the extent of Communist infiltration in the Hollywood motion-picture industry.' The Committee used pro-Soviet movies (such as 'Mission to Moscow') made during the war and the left-leaning nature of the Screen Writers' Guild as the pretext for the investigation. Actors such as Gary Cooper, Robert Taylor and future president Ronald Reagan were called before the Committee to testify to their experiences with communists.

When Thomas asked screenwriter John Howard Lawson about the organizations to which he belonged, Lawson challenged the Committee's right to ask such questions. Thomas threatened him with contempt, asking: 'You know what has happened to a lot of people that have been in contempt of this Committee this year, don't you?' (Several witnesses with current or past connections to the Communist Party asserted their First Amendment rights and refused to testify. They were cited and convicted for contempt of Congress; the Supreme Court upheld the rulings and they spent time in jail.) Lawson responded: 'I am glad you have made it perfectly clear that you are going to threaten and intimidate the witnesses, Mr. Chairman.' Lawson was eventually removed from the stand for refusing to answer the Committee's signature question, 'Are you now, or have you ever been a member of the Communist Party?' [13 *pp. 289–95*].

The CPUS itself also came under direct government attack. On 20 July 1948, the party's leaders were indicted for violating the Smith Act of 1940, which made it illegal to 'teach, advocate, or encourage the overthrow or destruction of ... government by force or violence.' The prosecution was no doubt popular: a poll in 1947 indicated that 61 percent of the American people supported outlawing the Communist Party. The following year, they were found guilty, and in 1951 the Supreme Court also upheld that ruling, over the dissents of Justices Hugo Black and William O. Douglas.

These actions by the three branches of the federal government had an impact on the larger society. Although loyalty was not mandated by law for other jobs, it became an informal, privately-instituted requirement for some professions. At some colleges and universities, for example, professors were required to sign loyalty oaths. Many public schools did the same for their teachers. Fearing a public backlash, labor unions, in particular the Congress of Industrial Organizations (CIO)*, expelled not only individual communists but entire unions deemed to be dominated by communists.

While such violations of individual rights bear no resemblance to the systematic terror of Stalin's regime, they do constitute a serious blot on the American civil liberties record. One of the founding principles of the United States is its devotion to the idea of the free exchange of ideas, confident that the best ideas will prevail in the contest. The red scare revealed the basic insecurity behind America's postwar bravado. A nation truly confident of both its power and the truth of its guiding ideals would not have felt compelled to stifle political expression, no matter how offensive those ideas might have been. The United States was not such a nation in the Truman years.

CHAPTER EIGHT

THE 1948 CAMPAIGN

By the time of the presidential campaign in 1948, anti-communism had become a bipartisan issue. The combination of Truman's foreign policy of containment and his domestic loyalty program had alienated the far left wing of the Democratic Party, which followed former vice-president Henry Wallace. Truman read Wallace out of the Democratic Party, and in a St Patrick's Day address in 1948 the president denounced him in the strongest possible terms: 'I do not want and I will not accept the political support of Henry Wallace and his Communists.' Wallace's presence in the race (he would seek the presidency on the Progressive Party ticket) allowed Truman to claim the political middle ground where American elections are generally won. He was more moderate than the Republicans on HUAC, but not an 'appeaser' like Wallace [79 p. 137].

Truman's tactic of using Wallace in this fashion epitomizes his campaign as a whole. The president was able to turn what seemed like negatives into positives. Heading into the campaign, Truman's position looked nearly hopeless. He was an accidental president, one who followed the all-time electoral champion, the four times elected Franklin Roosevelt. His performance as president had impressed few observers, even within his own party. He was blamed for allowing the Republicans to recapture control of Congress for the first time since the Hoover administration. In early 1947, it looked as if Truman might get as little as one-third of the popular vote. Wallace's expected candidacy might siphon off left-wing votes, a revolt by conservative southern Democrats threatened to cost Truman the 'solid South,' and Republicans were anticipating with glee the prospect of building on their 1946 successes and ending their 20 years in the political wilderness by recapturing the White House. Other than the president himself, few people thought that Truman had any real chance of winning election in his own right.

Of course, Harry Truman had the last laugh once the election results were in. Sporting his widest grin, he held aloft the *Chicago Tribune* with its famously incorrect headline, 'Dewey Defeats Truman.' Ever since, Truman has been the patron saint of every political underdog, the man who defied the polls and won the greatest upset in American history. While Truman's victory was certainly an upset, it was no miracle. It came as a result of a well-conceived campaign plan which accentuated the president's political strengths, capitalized on the weaknesses of his adversaries, and converted negatives into positives [52; 134; 139].

DEWEY AND THE REPUBLICANS

An understanding of the election outcome in 1948 requires analysis of the state of both political parties in the aftermath of the 1946 Congressional elections. The conventional wisdom of resurgent Republicans and declining Democrats exaggerated both Republican strengths and Democratic weaknesses. To be sure, there was some truth to that generalization. The extent of recent Democratic dominance was bound to lead to voter backlash at some point, and 1946 had shown that Republican themes once again resonated with a public for which the Depression was receding into memory. FDR's New Deal coalition seemed to be fracturing without his charismatic leadership to hold its many diverse interests together.

What was not quite as obvious, but just as meaningful, was the division within the outwardly unified Republicans. On both domestic and foreign policy, there were meaningful rifts within the Republican Party. A significant faction of the party was still reluctant to accept the permanency of the limited welfare state* created by FDR and wary of Truman's peacetime internationalism, particularly its emphasis on Europe (the prewar isolationists would emerge more clearly as the 'Asia First'* group in coming years). Others were increasingly convinced that continued opposition to popular programs like Social Security (in particular any talk of repeal) was political suicide, and preferred to mute their criticism of the New Deal and argue that Republicans would be more frugal and fiscally responsible in managing the welfare state. On foreign policy, the moderate wing, led by the convert to internationalism Senator Vandenberg, co-operated with and supported the Truman administration's major initiatives: aid to Greece and Turkey and the Marshall Plan. As a result, the Republican platform made little mention of foreign policy, maintaining for the time being the bipartisan moment and indulging only in some minor criticism of Democratic indecisiveness. Confident that they would win the White House, they felt no need to take potentially unpopular or controversial positions, particularly if they might leave the party open to charges of undermining the nation's international position.

The leading candidate for the nomination was the party's 1944 standard bearer, New York governor and former prosecutor Thomas Dewey. Dewey had taken on the thankless task of opposing FDR in the midst of World War

II, and had earned the right to an easier campaign. He fended off challenges from Robert Taft and Harold Stassen and captured the nomination. Dewey was from the more moderate wing of the party, a supporter of administration foreign policy and resigned to the New Deal. In some ways, his policies may have been closer to Truman's than to those of his own party. Dewey was thus in an awkward position. As representative of the whole party, he had to be careful not to alienate his own base by saying anything controversial. In retrospect, Dewey has received criticism for campaigning on platitudes. Most critics have explained this mistake by referring to Dewey's complacency about his ultimate victory, and no doubt that played a role. However, Dewey also had reason to be concerned about his own divided party. By speaking in generalities about how he would fix the mess the Democrats had made, Dewey could be all things to all Republicans [*Doc. 14*].

TRUMAN'S STRATEGY

The Democrats were also divided, and their divisions were open and obvious. Ironically, what seemed at first a severe handicap turned out to be an advantage for Truman. The overt disagreements in the party created the opportunity for Truman to seize the moderate middle, while banishing as extremists those most opposed to his renomination. Rather than smoothing over the rough spots, as Roosevelt had done, the more plain-spoken Truman would exacerbate them. His blunt style exposed the disagreements within the party, while he used his enormous inherent capacity as president to set the national agenda and also to define Democratic orthodoxy. When the dust cleared, Truman had survived the challenges to his party leadership.

Truman's strategy was outlined in a campaign memo by his aide Clark Clifford. The talented young Missourian, who had risen from being Truman's naval aide to an important presidential advisor in less than two years, began by noting the strains within the party: 'the Democratic Party is an unhappy alliance of Southern conservatives, Western Progressives and Big City labor.' The goal of the coming campaign was to get as many of the members of these disparate groups to vote Democratic on election day. Although Clifford mistakenly assumed that Truman could count on the 'solid South,' the remainder of his analysis was sound [*Doc. 13*].

The disappointment with Truman in the party's left wing reached a crescendo with the president's dismissal of Wallace in September 1946. Clifford noted in his memo that the expected Wallace candidacy presented a challenge. The trick for Truman was to marginalize Wallace, and thus give the most pragmatic liberals no choice but to return to the fold and support their president. If Wallace insisted on running, it would be necessary 'to identify and isolate him in the public mind with the Communists' [*Doc. 13*].

Wallace declared his independent candidacy in December 1947, and as noted above, Truman publicly associated him with the Communists. Wallace's foreign policy positions, particularly his opposition to the Truman Doctrine and his reversal of his initial support for the Marshall Plan, made Truman's job a relatively easy one. The escalation of the cold war had led many liberal and mainstream Democrats into the anti-communist camp, a trend manifest in the creation of Americans for Democratic Action (ADA)*. The ADA, while critical of Truman's domestic leadership, supported his anti-communist foreign policy and opposed Wallace's vision of co-operation with the Soviets. When the Communist Party in Czechoslovakia seized power in February 1948, most liberals were alarmed enough to reject Wallace and stay in the Democratic fold.

It was not enough for Truman to dissuade liberals from voting for Wallace; he had to give them a reason to vote for him. He reverted to rhetoric reminiscent of Roosevelt's attacks on the 'economic royalists' in the 1930s. Truman raised the class issue in the summer of 1947, when he successfully vetoed two Republican tax cuts, charging that they were give-aways to the wealthy. 'An adjustment of the tax system should provide fair and equitable relief for individuals,' Truman said in his veto message. 'A good tax bill would give a greater proportion of relief to the low income group' [*Doc. 9*]. Campaigning in Pontiac, Michigan in September 1948, Truman told his audience that the Republicans 'have given tax relief to the rich at the expense of the poor. They passed a rich man's tax law' [*7, 1948 p. 468*].

His State of the Union address in January 1948 was a liberal wish list, filled with proposals such as housing legislation which he well knew the Republicans in Congress would never approve. When they lived up to his expectations, he was able to blame Congress for its lack of action. Clifford specifically advised Truman to appeal to the 'atavistic fear ... of "Wall Street"' [*Doc. 13*]. This tactic would attract not only liberals but also southerners and westerners (especially farmers) who would be naturally suspicious of the New Yorker, Thomas Dewey. During the campaign, Truman dutifully denounced 'the Wall Street reactionaries [who] are attacking the whole structure of price supports for farm products' [*51 p. 153*].

Truman also had to mend fences with labor, and the Republican Congress inadvertently gave the president a golden opportunity to do so. In 1947, it passed the Taft–Hartley bill, which labor strongly opposed. The legislation, which passed over Truman's veto, gave the president authority to order an 80-day cooling-off period when the national interest demanded, outlawed the closed shop, allowed state right to work laws and federal injunctions against strikes, and required union leaders to swear that they were not communists. Truman's veto message called it 'a shocking piece of legislation. It is unfair to the working people of this country' [*Doc. 10*]. The veto was popular with labor, while the legislation was popular with the public at large. Thus labor was grateful to Truman that he had defended its interests, while the public felt content that unions had had their wings clipped. In a Labor Day address, Truman pointedly warned workers that Taft–Hartley was just the beginning of what Republicans had in store for labor if they gained the White House.

Clifford also noted that it was important to hold on to the votes of African-Americans, Jews, and ethnic Catholics, all of whom played an important role in FDR's coalition. Clifford observed that the black vote in the north 'holds the balance of power in Presidential elections.' The migrations northward during the two world wars had created powerful voting blocs in major cities in northern states rich in electoral votes. He urged 'new and real efforts (as distinguished from mere political gestures)' to cultivate their votes. The Jewish vote was key to winning New York, and Clifford noted the importance of Palestine to Jewish voters. However, he concluded that the issue should be 'approached on a basis of reaching decisions based upon intrinsic merit' rather than 'political expediency' [*Doc. 13*]. The Catholic vote, Clifford assumed, would be attracted by the president's hard line against communism as represented by the Truman Doctrine, because the Church was vehemently anti-communist. Following the script, in an appearance in Chicago near the end of the campaign, Truman appealed to all three groups and spoke of 'Dangerous men, who are ... attacking Catholics and Jews and Negroes and other minorities and religions' [*51 p. 155*].

In part due to the explicitly political nature of Clifford's advice, some historians have seen Truman's civil rights stand in 1948 and his decision to recognize the state of Israel as calculated decisions designed to improve the president's chances for re-election. There is certainly circumstantial evidence to support that view. On 29 June 1947, he became the first president to address the National Association for the Advancement of Colored People (NAACP). Truman privately confided to his sister that 'I wish I didn't have to make' the NAACP speech due to the divisive nature of the topic, but also said 'I believe what I say and I'm hopeful we may implement it' [*54 p. 433*].

In his NAACP address, Truman forcefully advocated vigorous enforcement of civil rights, arguing that the federal government must become 'a friendly, vigilant defender of the rights of all Americans. And again I mean all Americans' [*Doc. 11*]. That fall, the Civil Rights Committee appointed by Truman issued its report, *To Secure These Rights*. Its controversial recommendations included desegregation of the armed forces, a voting rights act, and permanent federal civil rights enforcement offices. Truman came out for civil rights by endorsing the report and submitting civil rights proposals to Congress in February 1948, though the administration did little to press Congress to pass the package, knowing that southern opposition made success virtually impossible.

On the surface, these steps might seem purely political. However, one must take into consideration the political costs of these steps as well. Truman's proposals were unpopular with the general electorate; whatever gains he might expect among black voters he might well have lost among whites. To be sure, many of the lost votes would be in the South, which Clifford assumed was safe. Nonetheless, Truman did make himself vulnerable there, and at the Democratic convention in the summer of 1948, Strom Thurmond of South Carolina led a walkout and launched an independent campaign under the Dixiecrat Party*. As the descendant of Missouri slave owners (his own mother evidently loathed Lincoln), Truman surely knew the depth of the reaction his civil rights proposals would provoke among southerners. No elected leader is completely immune to the political consequences of his actions, but on this issue, Truman's private confidence to his sister ('I believe what I say') is the most persuasive explanation of his decisions. To give his critics their due, however, one must note that Truman's most concrete action on civil rights, the executive order ending segregation in the armed forces, came on 30 July 1948, after the Dixiecrat revolt.

Truman's decision to recognize the state of Israel in May 1948 is also the subject of skeptical interpretations [145]. The State Department, to which Truman usually deferred, argued strenuously against recognition, fearing the effect it would have on American relations with Arab states in the Middle East. Secretary of State George Marshall himself made the case to Truman. The argument for recognition came from none other than Clark Clifford, which led Marshall to conclude that the movement to recognize Israel was motivated more by politics than national interests. He even warned Truman that he would not vote for the president if he overruled the State Department, but Truman did just that [4]. Given Truman's high regard for Marshall (there was likely no living American for whom he had more respect), the decision was certainly a difficult one. Reasonable observers can and have concluded that Truman's concern for the Jewish vote in November motivated him, but Dean Acheson (Marshall's successor as Secretary of State) concludes in his memoirs that this 'was not true.' Acheson observes that Truman 'held deep-seated convictions on many subjects,' and this was one such case [1 *p. 169*].

Regardless of whether these decisions were motivated by political calculation, they certainly had political consequences. Truman's conscious effort to woo important New Deal constituencies paid off. By the time the Democrats met for their convention, they had come to the conclusion (reluctantly in many cases) that for better or worse, they were stuck with Truman. Flurries of interest in drafting General Dwight D. Eisenhower or Supreme Court Justice William O. Douglas fizzled. Wallace was too far left and had no chance of winning; neither did Thurmond. Only Truman remained, and with a distinct lack of enthusiasm, most Democrats came home.

THE CAMPAIGN

The 1946 election débâcle had the effect of exposing the divisions within the Democratic Party and, contrary to expectations, that exposure proved salutary (the Republican success, on the other hand, left the party complacent and content to paper over its differences, much to its detriment). The open split with Wallace's Progressives and Thurmond's Dixiecrats meant that Truman had little need to court the political extremes in his own party. Instead, he could focus on the mainstream Democrats and independents (and potentially the moderate Republicans as well). Unlike Dewey, who had to keep happy the right wing led by Taft, Truman could openly reject Wallace and distance himself from Thurmond's anti-civil rights crusade. He could claim the moderate middle for himself. He could attack Dewey by attributing to him the most extreme views of the Republican coalition, leaving Dewey with the unenviable choice of remaining silent or repudiating the views of many Republicans. On the campaign trail Truman told his audiences that the Republicans would like to repeal the New Deal. How could Dewey respond? If he embraced the New Deal, he would alienate his own base; if he did not answer, Truman's charge stood unopposed. Dewey remained silent.

Harry Truman was anything but silent during his campaign. Seemingly drawing strength and energy from his underdog status, Truman revealed his aggressive style at the end of the convention which nominated him. Departing from the staid, awkward manner that marked his presidential speeches, Truman in his acceptance speech adopted the scrappy, folksy campaign style which he would make famous in the coming months. Reveling in the partisan setting, Truman challenged what he liked to call 'the do-nothing 80th Congress' to come back to Washington to pass the legislation their platform said they favored, a fairly liberal laundry list designed to appeal to Democratic voters. Confident that they would not act, Truman said that Congress 'can do this job in 15 days if they want to do it.' When Congress did not, Truman had made his point: the Republican Party did not favor liberal legislation, it was still the party of Hoover and the Depression [*Doc. 15*].

Despite all of these efforts, and a grinding campaign schedule, the nearly universal opinion was that the election was a foregone conclusion. Truman was credited with making a good show of it, but few people doubted that he would lose. At times, Harry Truman seemed to be the only person who believed he had a chance. Even as the crowds at his appearances grew, the prevailing opinion was that while Truman was clearly gaining ground, he simply had too far to go. In fact, it is clear in retrospect that things were not so dire. The last Gallup poll, taken in mid-October, showed Dewey with a five point lead. The poll indicated that Dewey was ahead and was likely to gain a strong electoral vote majority. Still, given the relatively undeveloped state of polling in 1948 and the time still to go before election day, it hardly guaranteed a Dewey victory.

When the results were in, Truman had done it. Truman won by the same margin in the popular vote by which he trailed in the last poll, five percent (49.5 percent to 44.5). He won a solid victory in the electoral college, taking 303 votes to Dewey's 189. The two other candidates, Wallace and Thurmond, each received about 2.5 percent of the vote, but since Thurmond's vote was concentrated in the south, he won 39 electoral votes while Wallace received none.

Truman had succeeded in reviving Roosevelt's coalition. Despite his difficulties with unions early on, the labor vote came out for Truman. So did the farm vote. Outside New York City, where Wallace ran strongly, Truman held on to the liberal urban vote. Blacks, Jews and Catholics went for Truman as well. The one trouble spot was the south. While Truman won most of the states of the former Confederacy, Thurmond managed to win four southern states. While that did not spell disaster for Truman, it was a foreshadowing of developments which would eventually tear apart the New Deal coalition. Continuing identification with civil rights would in time erode Democratic strength in the south, and make Republicans competitive there in the 1960s, for the first time since the end of Reconstruction* in 1877.

While Truman's whistle-stop train campaign is often credited with reviving his seemingly doomed campaign, the impact of style should not be overestimated. Certainly, by being more himself on the campaign trail, Truman came across as an approachable figure unlike the reserved, stiff and proper Dewey. The common people could easily identify with 'Give 'em hell, Harry.' In the final analysis, however, Truman's come-from-behind victory was not a triumph of style alone. Many factors contributed to the result, not the least of which was a robust economy. Unemployment stood at a mere two percent in 1948, and the inflation of the first Truman years had abated significantly. Despite this sunny economic picture, Truman received less than half of the popular vote, and won by the smallest margin since Woodrow Wilson's re-election in 1916.

Truman won by combining his combative personal style with a stout defense of Democratic accomplishments since 1933. Franklin Roosevelt created an unwieldy coalition, but it was a powerful one nonetheless. By turning the campaign into a referendum on the New Deal (i.e., the past), Truman played to the party's inherent strength. He reminded people of why they elected FDR president four times, what he had done, and by implication, what Hoover and the Republicans had failed to do (and had opposed). For example, speaking in Pontiac, Michigan on September 6, he reminded a labor audience that in '1932 we were in the worst depression in history. Labor was bearing the brunt of it.' But Democratic rule had changed all that: 'People can get jobs now at decent wages, and there are more jobs than there are people to take them.' He listed the accomplishments of the New Deal, and the attacks upon it by the 80th Congress: 'just a sample of what they would do if they had a Republican president who would go along with a Republican Congress' [7, 1948 *pp. 468–9*]. Truman was no FDR, as his critics often pointed out and his narrow victory attests, but he also was no Hoover. In 1948, with the postwar boom taking shape, and with the opposition offering a bland, cautious candidate, that was enough.

Truman's decision to reconstitute the New Deal coalition in 1948 and run on the New Deal record was a natural one, but in the end it was also a costly one. It served its immediate purpose and got Harry Truman elected president. The failure to make a strong case for the future, however, left Truman with little mandate to advance the New Deal in meaningful ways during the next four years. Instead, his election became a call for the preservation of the *status quo*. That underlying reality would hamstring Truman's domestic political ambitions in his next term, and produce stalemate rather than a revival of reform. In addition, by smearing Wallace with the charge of communism, Truman inadvertently discredited the domestic liberalism which Wallace also represented, giving conservatives more ammunition to attack reform proposals as 'communistic.' Arguably, the only area in which Truman proposed a substantial departure from the New Deal was in his civil rights package, and that was not going anywhere in the new Congress due to continuing southern opposition. His advocacy went a long way toward committing his party to civil rights, but as Thurmond's campaign demonstrated, it also exposed perhaps the deepest fault line in the Democratic Party.

The strategy also cost the Democratic Party in the long run. In 1948, Truman convinced the voters that Dewey and the Republicans could not be trusted with Roosevelt's legacy. Just as the 1946 election caused significant soul-searching in the Democratic Party, so would 1948 bring great changes in the Republican Party. They would draw lessons from their defeat, one of which would be felt almost immediately. In retrospect, Dewey's decision to avoid making foreign policy a campaign issue would seem a colossal error. Republicans would soon begin to abandon the bipartisan approach to foreign policy, with disastrous consequences for the Truman administration. (When Truman charged Dewey with being an isolationist near the end of the campaign, Dewey countered by referring to the number of people lost to communism under Truman, a small hint of things to come.) The party would also see the futility of overt opposition to the New Deal. Four years later, they would make their peace with what Roosevelt wrought, and nominate a man who would be seen as a non-political unifier who could lead the Grand Old Party (GOP) back to power.

In a larger sense, the Republican and Democratic parties were each going through a similar process during the Truman years. In both parties, those who seemed 'extreme' were becoming increasingly marginalized by the mainstream of the parties. The polarization which marked the politics of the mid-1930s was rapidly receding, being replaced by a move to the center by both major parties. A new consensus was emerging: a firm anti-communist internationalism in foreign policy and the maintenance (but not expansion) of the New Deal at home. This new consensus would reign until the mid-1960s, when the events of that tumultuous decade would destroy the cold war consensus which Harry Truman helped to create.

PART THREE

CHAPTER NINE

THE FAILURE OF THE FAIR DEAL

Truman's stunning re-election in 1948 marked the high point of his popularity. In political terms, he peaked at just the right time. He would never again during his presidency be as popular with the American people. The high hopes that his election created among Democrats were soon dashed, wrecked by the effects of the cold war at home and abroad. Truman was unable to translate his victory into a mandate for change. In fact, his election turned out to be, more than anything else, a vote for the *status quo*. He had campaigned and was elected as the defender of the New Deal. His second term saw the emergence of what has been called the 'liberal consensus*' of the 1950s, in which Democrats and Republicans came to a tacit agreement: the New Deal would neither be repealed nor dramatically expanded.

A *STATUS QUO* MANDATE

The liberal consensus represented mainstream American opinion. Democratic Party control of Congress (54–42 in the Senate, 263–171 in the House) did not equal liberal control – just as it had not since the New Deal effectively ended in 1938. Republicans and conservative southern Democrats continued to exert practical control of Congress. Now that the Democrats were back in the majority, many of the most important Congressional committees were once again controlled by southern Democrats. Ever since the end of Reconstruction, the southern states had effectively been one-party states. Democratic nominees faced no significant Republican opposition. The Democratic dominance of the south meant that most southern Democrats, once elected to office, held those positions for many years. Since the Congress ran on a seniority basis, and the longest-serving members were often southerners, those southern Democrats held tremendous power in the committees, where a determined chair could single-handedly kill a piece of legislation. It was this reality which led to FDR's caution on civil rights; Truman's civil rights advocacy in 1948–49 alienated those same southern Democrats, whose support for his agenda was essential. Therefore, there was little chance for any meaningful revival of reform beyond what the most conservative wing of the Democratic Party was willing to support.

Truman's 'Fair Deal' tried to do so nonetheless. Perhaps reading more into his election than the facts warranted, Truman proposed to Congress an ambitious liberal agenda in his January 1949 State of the Union address [*Doc. 16*]. It was similar to his September 1945 speech [*Doc. 3*]. He called for expanded Social Security coverage (the program had not been revised since 1939), national health insurance, an increase in the minimum wage from 40 to 75 cents an hour, the repeal of the Taft–Hartley Act*, the creation of a Department of Welfare, new TVA-style* public works projects, an immigration bill, public housing, a farm program, a permanent FEPC, an anti-lynching law, the abolition of poll taxes, and a $4 billion tax increase to finance these programs and reduce the national debt. The only significant recognition of the way in which the emerging consensus had moved away from the New Deal was Truman's emphasis on economic growth and the leading role of the private sector in creating jobs (as opposed to New Deal-style government work programs). This was a significant step away from the full employment proposal of the early Truman administration, and would become typical of postwar liberalism.

The president's program was met with a distinct lack of public enthusiasm. Liberals were pleased, but they did not have the votes to pass Truman's most ambitious proposals. That is not to say that Truman did not get some of what he asked from Congress; he did. In fact, in some ways, the 81st Congress was the most productive in years, at least since the late 1930s. It passed a housing bill (which provided for federal subsidies for 800,000 low-income housing units, though only half were actually built), slum clearance, urban renewal, the minimum wage increase, and approved some public works money. Most significantly, in August 1950 Congress passed a revision of Social Security which extended coverage and increased benefits, which one historian argues was almost as significant as the original 1935 legislation [*54 p. 506*]. Nonetheless, even this liberal success was compromised due to conservative power in Congress. Truman asked that coverage be extended to all 25 million workers not currently covered by the program; the legislation passed by Congress added millions to the rolls, but still left nearly 25 percent of American workers outside the system.

However impressive those accomplishments might be, what all of these bills had in common was that they broke no new ground. Each merely built upon previous reforms which had already achieved broad public acceptance and approval. All of Truman's proposals to carve out new responsibilities for the federal government were rebuffed: aid to education, national health insurance, and the permanent FEPC. The example of Truman's health insurance proposal is instructive. Within weeks of the State of the Union address, the proposal was already facing strong, organized opposition from the American Medical Association. The AMA began a nationwide public relations campaign to defeat the idea of 'compulsory health insurance,' calling for the publication and distribution of 100 million pamphlets to make their case. Critics denounced the health insurance proposal as 'socialized medicine' (a deadly epithet in the midst of the cold war) and the bill never made it out of committee. Similarly, Senate filibusters killed all attempts at civil rights legislation. The attempt to repeal the Taft–Hartley Act and the $4 billion tax increase also cut against the conservative grain and went down to defeat [124].

Noting the resistance to his program and increasingly distracted by foreign affairs, Truman did not push his liberal program terribly hard. Although the most outspoken liberals were frustrated that the feisty Truman of the campaign seemed nowhere to be found in 1949, the president knew that rallying the public was often easier than convincing conservative Congressmen of both parties to vote for legislation which they strongly opposed. Truman could also take some comfort in knowing that his administration blunted and frustrated the attack on Roosevelt's legacy, and had institutionalized the New Deal's reforms, so that they were no longer merely emergency measures prompted by depression and war. In the end, Truman made his stand on the most popular and therefore defensible liberal ground – preservation of the New Deal *status quo*. And, he could tell himself, he could always appeal to the people again in 1950, and perhaps have a more agreeable Congress after the next elections. He could not have known how events would conspire against him.

COLD WAR LIBERALISM

Despite Truman's victory in 1948, New Deal liberalism was in retreat in 1949. Truman's campaign had itself played a part in the process. Although the tactics used against Henry Wallace were targeted at his foreign policy which questioned the wisdom of containment, Truman inadvertently made common cause in this case with conservative enemies of domestic reform. The foreign policy debate of 1947–48 divided the New Deal coalition, and the Truman administration had worked with the same bipartisan group in Congress which opposed domestic reform: Republicans and conservative southern Democrats. The Republican Senator Arthur Vandenberg and the Texas Democratic Senator Tom Connally were the administration's allies in getting Congressional support for the Truman Doctrine and Marshall Plan. If Truman was going to get Congress to go along with his vision of American peacetime international leadership, he had no other choice. In the campaign, he continued his attack on the Wallace wing of the party for its 'appeasement' of the Soviet Union.

Wallace was more than an opponent of containment, however; he also represented the most liberal wing of the New Deal coalition, those most likely to favor Truman's Fair Deal. When his campaign rhetoric identified

Wallace with the Communists, Truman not only discredited Wallace's foreign policy but by extension liberal reform as well. Critics like Republican Senator Robert Taft argued that New Deal-style big government was just a step away from Soviet-style economic planning: 'The New Dealers really attacked the basic philosophy of American government, its belief in individual and local freedom, in competition and in reward for incentive. They echoed the arguments of Moscow against it, and wanted to move our system well over toward that of Russia' [*Doc. 12*]. As noted above, opponents attacked national health insurance as 'socialized' medicine. Civil rights crusaders were labeled 'Communists.' It is true that Truman himself never made these associations, and would have rejected them outright. Still, by sometimes employing the same rhetoric as his conservative political opponents, the president legitimized it, and increased the likelihood that it later would be turned against his own initiatives.

The tactic of red-baiting, whether by Truman or the Republican right, combined with the sobering realities of the cold war, had the effect of muting liberal voices. For example, in May 1949, the liberal Congress of Industrial Organizations (CIO) withdrew from the World Federation of Trade Unions due to the latter's association with the Soviet Union and its opposition to the Marshall Plan. Seeking to shed its leftist reputation, the CIO also endorsed NATO [168]. The cold war convinced liberals of the need to prove their toughness lest they fade into political oblivion. Wallace's critics had called him other-worldly, impractical, and naive. If liberalism was to survive, it needed to prove that it was none of these things. Arthur Schlesinger, Jr., one of the leading members of the ADA, published *The Vital Center* in 1949. In that work, the Harvard historian argued that liberals must be strongly anti-communist, and demonstrate the virility of liberalism. In urging liberals to cast off the illusions which led many blindly to support Stalin in the 1930s and during the war, the anti-communism of cold war liberals also implied a more realistic, practical approach to domestic problems [8].

Overall, liberalism had to temper the inspiring visions of the 1930s: peace and co-operation abroad, social and economic justice through enlightened political leadership at home. The world war inspired hopes that peace would bring a new age of international co-operation. The cold war proved that an illusion. Faced with the horrors of Stalinism, postwar liberals emerged from the experience chastened, with a greater appreciation for the darker side of human nature. This point of view, epitomized by the works of the theologian Reinhold Neibuhr, saw a world in which conflict at home and abroad was a necessary, inevitable part of life. If the problems of the world could only be managed, not solved, what did that say about liberal hopes for remaking society at home?

Doubts began to sap some of the enthusiasm for the progressive project. Reacting against radicalism of the left and the right, the new postwar libera-

1. Aside from this photo opportunity, Truman had little contact with Franklin D. Roosevelt during the former's brief vice-presidency, but the Truman presidency would institutionalize many of the changes begun under FDR.

2. All smiles on the occasion of General Dwight D. Eisenhower's retirement as Chief of Staff in February 1948, Truman and Ike would become political adversaries when Eisenhower ran for president as the Republican nominee in 1952.

3. In an unusual meeting on Wake Island in October 1950, Truman congratulates MacArthur for the successful Inchon landing in Korea. Six months later, the president would fire the popular general for publicly questioning the administration's war strategy in Korea.

4. Thrust into the presidency with little foreign policy experience or knowledge of FDR's diplomacy, Truman's years in office were dominated by world affairs. Here the new president meets with Winston Churchill and Joseph Stalin at the Potsdam Conference in

lism rejected extremes, adopted an anti-communist realism in foreign policy, and a consensus approach to politics at home. As a result, reform lacked a certain urgency. If reform was no longer a moral imperative, now more a question of management than transformation, what was the hurry? The New Deal had done the essential work. It had created a social safety net. Certainly it could be improved, and liberals would work hard to expand it. But the work which remained amounted at most to tinkering with the existing machinery of government, making it run more efficiently. The continuing prosperity of the postwar years also reduced the perceived need for further government action. Perhaps now the growing economy could provide fairly for all, and could eliminate the remaining pockets of poverty. The successes of the Truman agenda of 1949–50 represent the triumph of this less ambitious cold war liberalism.

Thus, although Truman saw much of his domestic program rejected by Congress, what he was able to achieve was enough for most moderate Democrats. Moreover, he and they could take heart in two cold war foreign policy successes in the spring of 1949: the end of the Berlin blockade and the signing of the North Atlantic Treaty. These triumphs would be the last good news Truman would receive for quite some time, and marked the high water mark of bipartisan foreign policy. Within months, events would shatter American confidence and leave many worrying that the United States was losing the cold war.

THE NORTH ATLANTIC TREATY ORGANIZATION

The second term began with early good news. Within days of Truman's inauguration, the administration received indications that the Soviet Union, which was still blockading Berlin, was tiring of the confrontation and looking for a way out. Ever since the previous June, American planes had been supplying West Berlin day and night. At last, American patience and perseverance were paying off. Negotiations ensued, and on 4 May 1949, the four occupying powers signed an agreement that the blockade (and western counter-blockade) would end on 12 May. The original Soviet purposes, either to drive the western allies out of Berlin or stop the formation of an independent West Germany, had failed. The western powers remained in Berlin, and on 8 May, a parliamentary council approved the constitution of the Federal Republic of Germany.

Adding to this victory for containment was the progress being made toward a formal military alliance between the United States and its western European friends. Talks began in 1948, but reached fruition in the spring of 1949. On 4 April, the United States and 11 other nations (Belgium, Britain, Canada, Denmark, France, Iceland, Italy, Luxembourg, the Netherlands, Norway and Portugal) signed the North Atlantic Treaty. The treaty declared that an attack on one member was an attack on all and required all members to come to the aid of a victim of aggression. Although such assistance did not necessarily mean that the United States would automatically go to war (nervous senators were assured that the right of Congress to declare war would not be affected), for all practical purposes, American membership in NATO assured that if war broke out in Europe, the United States would become immediately involved. Rising cold war tensions had understandably made western European leaders nervous about the prospects of a hot war breaking out. Given that the American reaction in each of the previous two world wars in the twentieth century had been to remain neutral for over two years before becoming a belligerent, they wanted assurances that history would not repeat itself. American membership in NATO gave them that assurance. In addition, the specter of American involvement meant that the Soviet Union had to be concerned that any military thrust into western Europe might well result in the use of atomic weapons against the Soviet Union itself – a powerful deterrent to war.

Careful consultations with the Senate assured that the treaty would not suffer the fate of Woodrow Wilson's League of Nations. Like the League, NATO contained a collective security provision. Unlike the League, NATO was limited to certain nations whose interests closely aligned with those of the United States and the treaty received widespread bipartisan support. In 1919, the United States was not prepared to take on the international role which Wilson envisioned. Thirty years and another world war (and cold war) later, that had changed. Over the course of two years, from the Truman Doctrine speech in March 1947 to the signing of the North Atlantic Treaty in April 1949, the Truman administration successfully made the case for American internationalism. (Recent Soviet actions in Czechoslovakia and Berlin certainly helped.) When the treaty came up for a Senate vote in July 1949, it passed easily, 82–13. Following up on its success, the administration asked Congress for $1.4 billion in military assistance to Europe [70].

The ratification of the North Atlantic Treaty was a milestone not only for the Truman administration, but in the history of American foreign relations. For nearly 150 years (since 1800, when the French alliance forged in the American Revolution was dissolved), the United States scrupulously had followed Washington's famous advice against involvement in entangling alliances. American participation in NATO was a sign that the United States had come to accept that a policy which served well a small, young and weak nation was no longer appropriate for a great world power.

The American decision to ally itself formally with the nations of western Europe was an unquestionable commitment to an internationalist foreign policy. The stationing of American troops in Europe was no longer merely the necessary aftermath of the war effort, but an ongoing, permanent presence. Moreover, regardless of the fact that Congress technically still held the power to declare war, the United States had committed itself to the defense of western Europe. Its troops would be on the front lines, and inevitably would be engaged in any combat as soon as it began. Unlike the first two world wars, if World War III came, the United States would not declare neutrality – it would immediately become a belligerent. After a century and a half of trying to isolate itself from European wars, the United States had come to the decision that the best way to avoid involvement would be to deter such a conflict in the first place. And, American leaders believed, the only way to do that would be to guarantee American involvement in the next war. That commitment, like NATO itself, would survive even the end of the cold war.

NATO also marked the high point of the bipartisan foreign policy. Senators of both parties supported the treaty and presented a united front to the Soviet Union and the world. Although it was not apparent at the time, that spirit of bipartisanship would soon be in tatters. Just three weeks after the Senate vote on NATO, the State Department issued its 'White Paper'* on recent American relations with China. The rancor and partisanship which that document unleashed would plague the Truman administration until its final days.

In the aftermath of his electoral victory, Harry Truman was unable to make bold new departures in domestic and foreign policy. What he did accomplish, however, was perhaps more significant in the long run. Truman built on the previous accomplishments of the Roosevelt administration and his own nearly full term as Roosevelt's successor. FDR had created the limited welfare state during a time of economic crisis; arguably, it could not have been done under any other circumstances. In World War II, Roosevelt presided over the elevation of the United States into a true world power, perhaps *the* world power. In that, of course, he had the advantage of acting in the context of a world war, one which Americans believed had been thrust upon them against their will.

Harry Truman's historical task was both easier and more difficult than that of his illustrious predecessor. He was building on the foundation created by FDR; he did not need to start from scratch. On the other hand, Truman needed to convince Americans that domestic reform measures enacted during the greatest economic disaster in the nation's history remained necessary in the midst of a great economic expansion. While FDR faced no significant opposition to American participation in World War II after the attack on Pearl Harbor, Truman had the job of convincing a reluctant public to commit itself to an ongoing, permanent role in international affairs at a time when it had unprecedented economic and military power. Just as Truman institutionalized the New Deal (which was born in depression) in times of prosperity, so too did he institutionalize internationalism (which was born in war) in time of peace.

CHAPTER TEN

THE COLLAPSE OF BIPARTISANSHIP

The price that Truman paid for his electoral and foreign policy successes became evident in the latter half of 1949. The rhetoric which he used so successfully against Wallace was now directed against the president, the fear which helped unite the country behind the internationalist foreign policy grew beyond his control as events around the world called into question the wisdom of his policies. The increasing intersection of domestic and foreign policy began to undermine support both for Truman's domestic and foreign policies. In some sense, Truman became a victim of his own success.

THE 'LOSS' OF CHINA

The trouble for Truman began with the collapse of Chiang Kai-shek's Nationalist (Guomindang) regime in China. Ever since the 1920s, Chiang had been competing with the Chinese Communist Party (CCP) for control of China. A forced, uneasy truce prevailed during the fight against Japan from 1937 to 1945, but the two rivals never truly made peace with each other. They well knew that when Japan was defeated, the war for control of China would begin. The United States supported Chiang throughout the war, and FDR tried to raise him and his weak, divided nation to great power status (best symbolized by his insistence that China be a permanent member of the United Nations Security Council). After the war, Truman's policy was to encourage a coalition between Chiang and the Communists, led by Mao Zedong. The CCP had gained patriotic credentials during the Japanese war by their effective resistance to Japanese control of China, while Chiang and his Nationalists were seen as biding their time until the Americans won the war for them, and hoarding their weapons and ammunition for the coming civil war, rather than taking on the Japanese.

American mediation efforts, led by General George Marshall, failed. The ancient nation descended into civil war. The United States aided Chiang's government, but it soon became apparent that no amount of aid could keep his government afloat. Sending American troops into China to save him was unthinkable, and thus the Truman administration reluctantly came to the conclusion that his was a lost cause. It reluctantly resigned itself to Mao's eventual triumph.

At that point the trap Truman had inadvertently laid for himself two years earlier was sprung. The language of the Truman Doctrine was universal in its implications. Its manichean world-view saw only two ways of life, and pledged that the United States would support those nations resisting aggression and subversion by totalitarian forces [*Doc. 8*]. In rallying the public to support peacetime internationalism, Truman did not distinguish between the nations of Europe and the rest of the world, he did not say that the United States would only come to the aid of those who had a chance to win. The Truman administration justified its decision to end aid to Chiang's regime as a refusal to throw good money after bad, but its critics saw something far worse: a willingness to *allow* the Chinese Communists to come to power in the world's most populous nation.

Republicans saw in the Truman administration's inability to save Chiang Kai-shek a political opening which they were quick to seize. In the aftermath of Dewey's defeat, it became apparent that the Republicans made a tactical error in largely avoiding foreign policy as an election issue. Confident of victory, Dewey saw no need to criticize policies which he mostly supported and which he expected essentially to continue when he became president. Truman's victory left the Republicans stunned and unwilling to give the president a pass on foreign policy. The retirement of the widely respected Secretary of State George Marshall, and his replacement by Dean Acheson, the brilliant but often caustic eastern establishment lawyer, made the Republican task that much easier. While the Republicans did not take their new adversarial approach so far as to torpedo the ratification of the North Atlantic Treaty (which they largely supported), they did lie in wait for a suitable opportunity to criticize the Democratic administration. China provided that opening [72].

Not only was the 'loss' of China of self-evident importance, but China also fitted Republican needs in another way. In the new internationalist era, many former isolationists within the GOP had found a way to continue their traditional aversion to American involvement in European intrigue by transforming themselves into 'Asia First' internationalists. They argued that the United States had been historically wise to avoid entanglement in European affairs, but had always taken an interest in Asia. They argued that America's past was in the west, its future was in the east. This group focused on China. They were part of a long tradition of Americans who felt a special attachment to China, who indulged in romantic notions of the United States as the protector of China against the rapacious imperialism of the European powers at the turn of the century [33]. They also believed in the omnipotence of the United States; if the United States did not want communism to triumph in China, it would not.

When Mao stood in Tianamen Square in October 1949 and proclaimed the People's Republic of China, the Republican Party had an issue to use against Truman. They charged that the administration had 'lost' China (begging the question of how the United States could lose a sovereign, independent nation which it did not 'have' in the first place). It had betrayed its own policy of containment and allowed communism to spread. If the United States supported Greece in 1947 and saved it from communist takeover, why had it failed to do so in the case of China? How could this happen?

At the same time, another equally if not more disquieting event occurred: the Soviet Union exploded an atomic device of its own, ending the American nuclear monopoly. In September 1949, President Truman announced to the stunned nation that radiation had been detected in the atmosphere which indicated that the Soviets now had atomic weapons. Only four years after the American achievement, the Soviets had equaled it. How could that be possible?

In the charged and fearful atmosphere of late 1949, one response seemed to explain both problems: the enemy within. If the Chinese communists had triumphed, it must be because the State Department was filled with sympathizers who allowed that to happen. If the Soviets had gotten the bomb, it must be because Americans gave them the secrets. In both cases, frightening international developments outside of the ability of the United States to control were made manageable again by attributing them not to uncontrollable forces, but by locating the source of the problem at home, where it could be rooted out and solved. If the problem was within, so was the solution. If the march of communism was abetted by communist sympathizers in the State Department, then it could be halted by removing those disloyal Americans. If Soviet technological advances were due to treachery by Americans, then they could be stopped by exposing the spies.

The Truman administration tried to explain these developments calmly and rationally. The China 'White Paper' examined the roots of the civil war in China, and concluded that events there were beyond the control of the United States. The 'secret' of the atom bomb was less of a secret than an engineering problem; American scientists always assumed that it was only a matter of time (perhaps five years) before the Soviets solved it. Some thought it might take longer, perhaps up to ten years, but none were under the illusion that only Americans could make an atomic bomb. Of course there was also atomic espionage during the war, which might well have accelerated the Soviet program, but that had long ago been ended [159].

Despite these reasonable responses, the seemingly sudden turn for the worse in the cold war reinvigorated the red scare. The major difference between this outbreak and the earlier one was the target: the Truman administration itself. Previously, the targets had been the Communist Party, specific individuals in and out of government, leftists of various stripes. With the

Communist Party increasingly a shell of its former self, with the left wing in the United States vanquished with Henry Wallace's poor showing in 1948, Truman and his government became the focus of the attacks.

McCARTHYISM

Moderate Democrats and cold war liberals were astonished that they could be accused of sympathy with communism. How could the Truman administration, which had taken a hard line against the Soviet Union, stand accused of being 'soft' on communism? It seemed to make no sense. Rationally, that was true. The upsurge in the red scare in 1950, which became known as 'McCarthyism*' after its most infamous practitioner, Wisconsin Republican Senator Joseph McCarthy, was not a rational phenomenon. It was rather an irrational attempt to reconcile the myth of American omnipotence with the undeniable reality of setbacks in the cold war. New Hampshire Republican Senator Styles Bridges captured the essence of the argument: 'Stalin is not a superman. He had to have help from inside our ranks' [72 *p. 76*]. In March 1950 McCarthy asked: 'How can we account for our present situation unless we believe that men high in this government are concerting to deliver us into disaster? This must be the product of a conspiracy' [32 *p. 376*].

As if Mao's triumph and Stalin's possession of the atomic bomb were not enough, the new year brought another blow to the administration. On 22 January 1950, a jury convicted former State Department official Alger Hiss on perjury charges arising out of his denial that he had been a Soviet agent in the late 1930s and during the war. The Hiss case grew out of investigations by HUAC, energetically pursued by the young Congressman from California, Richard Nixon. Acting on information supplied by former communist turned anti-communist Whittaker Chambers, Nixon doggedly hunted Hiss, gaining the Congressman lasting political friends among conservatives and the enduring enmity of liberals. Now a jury seemed to vindicate Nixon: Hiss had lied when he denied passing classified documents to the Soviets [158].

The Hiss case was particularly embarrassing for the Democrats. Hiss was the stereotypical eastern establishment liberal: well-born, well-educated, and well-connected. In short, he represented everything which conservatives loathed about eastern liberal elitism. His high profile as a New Dealer only clinched the case: not only did the New Dealers have socialist tendencies at home, they were disloyal as well. Secretary of State Dean Acheson, who was a friend of Donald Hiss, Alger's brother, compounded the administration's problems. He had vouched for Hiss's character, and when asked about the perjury conviction, Acheson cited a passage from scripture ('I was in prison and you came to me') and told reporters 'I do not intend to turn my back on

Alger Hiss.' Acheson's statement was an expression of personal loyalty, not approval of anything Hiss might have done. It was also a political disaster.

Such subtle distinctions were lost on the administration's opponents. Upon hearing of Acheson's statement, Republican senators were quick to tie the Hiss case to the issues of communists in government and the fall of China. Nixon charged that Hiss had been protected by high officials in the Roosevelt and Truman administrations. Senator Karl Mundt (a former HUAC member) sneered at Hiss's 'Harvard accent' and charged that he contributed to a policy 'which has resulted in the disastrous collapse of autonomous China and the complete domination of that once great ally of ours by the Moscow-supported armies of communism.' Senator McCarthy wondered if Acheson's statement indicated that 'he will not turn his back on any of the other Communists in the State Department?' [*Doc. 17*]. It did no good to point out that Hiss had been eased out of the State Department in 1946, and thus had been in no position to affect American foreign policy for nearly four years. The presence of Hiss at the Yalta Conference in February 1945 now became part of the explanation of how Poland and the rest of eastern Europe was 'sold out' to the Russians by FDR. Early the following month, McCarthy made his famous speech in Wheeling, West Virginia, in which he charged that there were 205 known communists working in the State Department. The McCarthyite witch hunt was on [113; 140].

Thus the Republican desire to attack Truman and the New Deal legacy merged with new cold war problems to create an unusual opportunity for the frustrated and disappointed Republican Party. By exaggerating both the threat of communism and the ability of the United States to counter its growth abroad, Truman oversold his policies and exposed himself to charges of negligence if not treason when things went sour. By arguing that the Soviet Union was the source of all revolutions, the administration undermined its own case when it maintained that the Chinese communists came to power by their own efforts and might not be mere tools of Moscow. It was in vain to argue, as Acheson did, that China was not Greece. In his view, true consistency lay not in acting the same way in every corner of the world, but in acting always in the best interest of the United States. Further attempts to prop up Chiang Kai-shek were useless, and thus not in the American interest [153].

The outrage of what became known as the 'China Lobby,' a group of political leaders, journalists and others who championed Chiang's cause in the United States, prevented reasonable debate on the subject. Their insistence that the United States continue to recognize the Nationalist government (now driven off the mainland on to the island of Taiwan) as the official government of all of China handcuffed the Truman administration in its dealings with China. The lack of an official channel for the two governments to communicate directly would have dire consequences later in 1950.

On Valentine's Day, 1950, the United States watched as the two communist giants consummated their courtship. Mao and Stalin agreed to a Sino-Soviet alliance, obligating each to aid the other in case of attack by Japan 'or any state allied with her,' a veiled reference of course to the United States [6 *p. 59*]. While seasoned observers might note that the two months Mao spent in Moscow seemed to indicate a certain inability to come to mutually agreeable terms, the formal agreement between the two powers added to the American sense of dread. In fact we now know that Stalin harbored a deep mistrust of Mao, and that traditional Russian–Chinese rivalry had not been obliterated by ideology. By the end of the 1950s, cracks would appear on the surface of the communist 'monolith,' which by the 1960s would become gaping chasms. In 1950, however, the world's largest country in land mass and the largest in population stood united under the banner of communism and in opposition to the capitalist west led by the United States.

THE MILITARIZATION OF THE COLD WAR

This potentially dramatic shift in the world balance of power alarmed members of the Truman administration. In the spring of 1949, American leaders could look at Europe with satisfaction. Marshall Plan aid was rapidly reviving the economies of western Europe, the airlift had kept alive the western presence in Berlin and demonstrated western resolve, and the United States and its allies had formalized their unity through NATO. By the following spring, however, American national security officials feared that the cold war was being lost, and that immediate reactions were required. Their response was a document called National Security Council Paper No. 68 (NSC-68)* [99].

The report to the president, dated 7 April 1950, was a far cry from the confident tone of George Kennan's Long Telegram. Unlike Kennan's analysis, which saw the Soviet Union as an aggressive power but one which was not bent on war, NSC-68 argued that 'the Kremlin seeks to bring the free world under its dominion.' While Kennan argued that the Soviets desired the fruits of war without going to war, NSC-68 maintained that it was 'seeking to create overwhelming military force, in order to back up infiltration with intimidation' [*Doc. 18*].

The more apocalyptic tone of NSC-68 derives from the same sources as the domestic red scare. It pointedly noted that Soviet military power was now enhanced by atomic weapons and that Mao's triumph in China gave them new opportunities to infiltrate and destabilize Asia. The long-term threat to the United States was that the Soviet Union might come to control enough territory and resources that the United States and its allies might be incapable of effectively countering it. The solution was a substantial rearmament by the United States and its allies.

Kennan's original concept of containment focused on the political and economic, targeting areas of primary importance to the United States. Now NSC-68 was elevating the military component of containment above the others. It called specifically for a 'substantial increase in expenditures for military purposes ... [and] military assistance programs,' while saying that economic assistance programs should receive only 'some increase.' Psychological warfare, covert action, improved intelligence activity, civil defense – all of these were part of the militarization of the cold war under NSC-68 [*Doc. 18*].

The document was largely the work of Secretary Acheson and the head of Policy Planning at the State Department, Paul Nitze. Acheson felt that the changed international circumstances required a revision of American policy, but he faced the steadfast opposition of his boss, President Truman. As a senator during the war, Truman made a national name for himself through his investigations of war manufacturers, exposing fraud and price-gouging. He continued to be suspicious of defense spending as president. He appointed a known cost-cutter, Louis Johnson, as Secretary of Defense. His budget plan for fiscal year 1950 was to limit defense spending to $14.3 billion and to cut it to $13.5 billion in fiscal 1951 to free up funds for his Fair Deal initiatives. Although it did not call for a specific dollar amount, NSC-68's call for 'substantial' increases was clearly at odds with Truman's plans.

NSC-68 did not shrink from the domestic consequences of its suggestions. It recognized that the spending levels it envisioned would require the '[r]eduction of Federal expenditures for purposes other than defense and foreign assistance, if necessary by the deferment of certain desirable programs,' as well as '[i]ncreased taxes.' In short, domestic spending would have to be sacrificed in the name of greater military preparedness in the escalating competition with the Soviet Union. The Fair Deal would be a casualty of the cold war [*Doc. 18*].

Truman refused at first to accept the stark choice his national security team presented to him. After reading it, he ordered that the secret document be handled with special care and that no part of it become public, and continued to say that he wanted to cut defense spending. He was not convinced that the cold war had taken this decidedly military turn or that it required such a significant reorientation of American priorities. There the matter stood, when on the evening of 24 June 1950, Dean Acheson phoned the president at his home in Independence, Missouri, and told him that the North Korean army had invaded South Korea.

CHAPTER ELEVEN

THE KOREAN WAR AND THE MILITARIZATION OF THE COLD WAR

The outbreak of war in Korea shifted the focus of containment from the political and economic to the military. Taken by surprise by this sudden invasion of pro-American South Korea by the communist North, the president and the rest of his administration came to the conclusion that a new and more dangerous stage of the cold war had begun. Faced with American resolve in Europe and the success of the political and economic aspects of containment in that theater, the Soviets had changed tactics and shifted their attention to Asia, the administration decided. The United States, Truman firmly believed, must meet this test as it had met the others which preceded it, lest it invite further aggression which could only result in a third world war [58; 148; 160].

This interpretation of events in Korea had profound consequences for how the United States viewed the cold war as a whole. The seemingly apocalyptic language of NSC-68 now struck even the president as prescient rather than alarmist. Secretary of State Acheson took the lead in pushing for NSC-68 and the militarization of the cold war. He argued that strengthening NATO was essential now that the cold war had turned hot. The invasion of South Korea convinced the president to endorse the conclusions of NSC-68.

The Korean War also led to the globalization of the cold war. As a result, more US troops (four additional divisions) were sent to Europe, and the administration began the rearmament of Germany. The defense budget, which stood at $17.7 billion in 1950, rose to $53.4 billion in 1951, that is, the higher levels sought by NSC-68. Only part of that increase was due to the cost of actual combat in Korea. Most of it went to rebuild and expand the US military.

The whole American approach to the cold war altered as a result of Korea. Previously, most American foreign aid was economic in nature, in the form of Marshall Plan assistance. Military aid was secondary. During the Korean War, those priorities changed places. In 1947, military aid by the United States to its allies totalled $97 million. By 1950, in part because of NATO, it had risen to $523 million. In 1952, however, it jumped to $2.7 billion. For the first time, military aid was greater than economic aid. From this point on, a confrontation which began in Europe would be played out all over the world: in Asia, the Middle East, Africa and Latin America. Containment, which was originally conceived as a means of guarding vital American interests in Europe and Japan, became a universal policy which applied to peripheral as well as vital interests. As NSC-68 put it, 'a defeat of free institutions anywhere is a defeat everywhere' [*Doc. 18*].

MEETING THE CHALLENGE

Ironically, all of these changes in American cold war policy may well be due to an erroneous US interpretation of the meaning of the North Korean invasion. The United States viewed events in Korea strictly through the lens of the cold war. The reality was more complex than that, however. Before and during World War II, Korea was a Japanese colony. With Japan's unconditional surrender in August 1945, arrangements had to be made to accept the surrender of Japanese troops in Korea. By virtue of the fact that the Soviets had declared war on Japan days earlier, the United States and Soviet Union decided to share that responsibility, with the Soviets accepting the surrender north of the 38th parallel, and the United States doing the same in the south. As in Germany, this division was originally intended to be temporary, but as the cold war escalated it solidified and became permanent.

US occupation forces tapped Syngman Rhee, a Korean nationalist, to head a pro-American government in the south. The United States forged ties with rightist and anti-communist elements in South Korea to thwart leftists who wanted to replace Rhee and unite with the communist north led by Kim Il Sung. With a seemingly secure government installed in the south, the United States began to look for a way to withdraw from Korea, given its many other important commitments elsewhere. The American withdrawal date of 30 June 1949 was preceded by a build-up of Rhee's army to resist a potential North Korean invasion. American aid was limited, however, by fears that if Rhee became too strong, he would make good on his threats to unite the country by force. Meanwhile, the Soviets built up the North Korea regime, supplying it with military equipment as well, despite Kim's open ambitions to unite Korea under *his* rule. The situation was an inherently unstable one. The nation was artificially and arbitrarily divided by two great powers, and each power installed a nationalist leader sympathetic to it but also ambitious to control the whole nation [34].

The Truman administration never considered the possibility that the decision to send the North Korean Army across the 38th parallel was made anywhere but in Moscow. The North Korean leader, Kim Il Sung, was a communist brought to power by Soviet forces after World War II. Therefore, the United States assumed that he was acting under orders from the Soviets. Recently released documents seem to paint a more complex picture of events, however. The initiative in fact seems to have come from Kim, not Stalin. While the Soviet leader did give Kim permission to invade South Korea (provided Mao also agreed), Stalin was evidently dubious of Kim's success, and told him that he was on his own if the United States intervened. While Stalin did continue to supply Kim's forces and helped plan the invasion, he was not willing to participate openly for fear of provoking the United States. Thus, the North Korean invasion was not part of a general Soviet offensive in the cold war.

In that sense, Truman and his advisors probably misinterpreted the meaning of the invasion. North Korean success did not necessarily mean that the United States could expect other aggressive acts in other areas, such as Europe. It was evidently an event of local, not global, import. On the other hand, to give the administration its due, Stalin's decision to give Kim the go-ahead (after having denied previous requests to invade) does suggest a somewhat more aggressive attitude by Stalin, perhaps due to his possession of the atomic bomb, his new alliance with the People's Republic of China, or both. Thus it is at least possible that had the United States not acted in this situation, Stalin might well have been tempted to test American resolve elsewhere.

The administration never seriously considered the idea of allowing the North Korean invasion to go unanswered. The United States saw the move as potentially damaging to Japan's security, and the former enemy had become the center of American policy in Asia once the communists triumphed in China. More significantly, the administration saw its credibility at stake. It might well be that Korea, in and of itself, was not important to American interests. However, Truman feared that if the United States did not help Rhee's government, which the United States had established, it might have an impact on the confidence of America's other allies. Would the Europeans, for example, begin to doubt the American commitment to NATO if the United States failed to act in Korea? The periphery must be defended lest adversaries be encouraged to challenge vital interests. Had not the Munich Conference of 1938 proven that, when Britain and France appeased Hitler by sacrificing Czechoslovakia but still failed to prevent World War II?

Inevitably, Truman must also have been concerned about the domestic political ramifications of a failure to respond to the North Korean attack. For nearly a year, the administration had been under withering fire from its opponents for standing by while Chiang's government in China fell. What would happen if Truman allowed Rhee to fall as well? Such an outcome could only add fuel to the already raging anti-communist fire that threatened to consume the administration. Having been accused of being soft on communism, Truman could not risk another cold war loss in Asia [114].

For all of these reasons, Truman decided immediately to respond. The United States got the UN Security Council to approve a resolution calling for repulsion of the North Korean invasion on 27 June, thus giving the United States the cover of international law and multilateral action (the Soviets were boycotting the UN over its refusal to seat Communist China and thus were not present to veto the American proposal). On 28 June, Truman ordered American air and sea power deployed against the North Koreans. He ordered the Seventh Fleet to position itself between mainland China and the island of Formosa (Taiwan), to which Chiang's Nationalists had fled in 1949. By so doing, Truman reinjected the United States into the Chinese conflict and *de facto* committed the United States to the protection of Taiwan, a commitment which would outlast the end of the cold war.

American air and sea power proved unable to stem the North Korean advance. On 30 June, General Douglas MacArthur, commander of American forces in Asia, told the administration that only American ground troops could save South Korea. Despite the use of US troops, by the end of July the North Koreans had soon driven American and South Korean forces down to the southeast tip of the peninsula, the so-called Pusan perimeter. It seemed possible that the American effort had been in vain. General MacArthur then proposed a bold plan: an amphibious invasion on the western coast of Korea, behind enemy lines, at Inchon. Some in the Pentagon called it a 5,000 to one shot. It was certainly a gamble, but MacArthur's tremendous prestige and the lack of a better plan led to its acceptance by the administration.

The Inchon operation, which began on 15 September, was a great success. MacArthur caught the North Koreans unprepared. The combination of the amphibious operation and a land offensive from the south sent the North Koreans reeling. Within weeks, the North Korean offensive became a retreat, and the administration found itself facing an altogether different dilemma. With the enemy on the run, should the US–South Korean offensive halt at the 38th parallel or pursue and destroy the enemy? The original purpose of the American intervention (and the UN mandate) was to repel the invasion. That goal had been accomplished. Now a more tempting prospect dangled in front of Truman and his advisors: rollback, liberation of a country once under communist rule. Critics had charged that containment was too defensive a policy, that it did not challenge communist control, but merely tried to prevent its spread. Here was an opportunity to go beyond containment to rollback. What better message to send to potential aggressors: not only will aggression be resisted and repelled, but the aggressor faces annihilation.

The prospect proved too tempting for Truman to ignore. After seeking and receiving reassurance from MacArthur that the communist Chinese, who shared a border with North Korea, would not intervene (or would be easily defeated if they did), Truman gave his commander the authority to cross the 38th parallel and destroy the North Korean Army. Success would mean the unification of all Korea under Syngman Rhee's pro-American government. What had seemed a dire threat to world peace and American interests just four months earlier had become an opportunity for the United States to score a dramatic victory in the cold war.

A WHOLE NEW WAR

It was not to be. MacArthur, supremely confident of his mastery of the situation, badly misjudged the Chinese. As the UN forces, dominated by the United States, drove north toward the Yalu River, which separated North Korea and the People's Republic of China, Mao Zedong in Beijing grew increasingly concerned. Lacking formal diplomatic relations with the United States, the Chinese sent word through third parties that they could not sit idly by and watch potentially hostile forces approach their border. In late October, scattered reports of Chinese 'volunteers' among the North Korean forces began to appear. Neither Truman nor MacArthur were concerned. The offensive continued. As CIA estimates of Chinese troops in North Korea rose to as much as 40,000 in November, the Joint Chiefs grew more cautious and raised the possibility that perhaps MacArthur should stop short of the Yalu. Confident of victory, MacArthur continued, promising to end the war and have the troops home for Christmas [162].

Instead, he encountered a massive Chinese intervention, perhaps 250,000 troops. His offensive was halted by their stiff resistance and now it was the American Army's turn to convert advance into retreat. As the Chinese–North Korean forces drove the battle lines once again south of the 38th parallel in December, the Truman administration was forced to reconsider its war plans. Chinese involvement had indeed created a new war. MacArthur argued that he should receive authority to take the war to the Chinese: bombing their territory, blockading their coast, invading their territory with Chiang's Nationalist forces. In short, MacArthur wanted to continue the policy of rollback. Rather than seeing the Chinese intervention as reason to be cautious, he saw it as an opportunity for an even greater liberation, that of China itself.

Back in Washington, an altogether different mood prevailed. Rollback seemed feasible and attractive when it only involved North Korea. The intervention of the communist Chinese altered everything. An American attack on China could trigger World War III. The Chinese were allies of the Soviets, after all. Not only that, but the Soviets now had atomic weapons (although their stockpile was limited to about 25 bombs and they did not have the capacity to strike the United States, they certainly could do tremendous damage to American allies in Europe and Asia). Any conflict thus threatened to escalate to nuclear war. However attractive rollback was, it was not worth the risk of world war [146].

The debate was an important one, and its outcome affected the course of military operations for the rest of the cold war. The American dilemma in Korea crystallized the problem with military operations in an age of nuclear weapons. In World War II, American policy was total war and unconditional surrender. MacArthur's proposals embodied that attitude. The new reality of the cold war, however, dictated that wars must be limited; if they were not, they threatened to escalate out of control with unthinkable consequences. The awful power of the atomic bomb required caution, not risk-taking. Future presidents throughout the cold war would face this dilemma: how to use military power to protect American interests without risking a conflict which threatened the most basic of interests, survival.

THE FIRING OF MACARTHUR

Once UN forces regained the offensive and the front again approached the 38th parallel, the Truman administration (with the support of its European allies, the likely targets of any Soviet offensive in a general war) decided not to seek total military victory, but instead pursue a negotiated peace which would restore the prewar *status quo*. MacArthur strongly disagreed, and made his disagreement public. He wrote a letter to the Republican Leader of the House which openly opposed Truman's policy. When the letter was made public on 5 April 1951, Truman had no choice but to dismiss the popular general. It was, as Truman wrote in his diary, 'Rank insubordination' [5 p. 210]. MacArthur in his zeal challenged not just this policy but the principle of civilian leadership of the military. No president could abide such public behavior, and Truman, who was keenly aware of his responsibility to the office he held, did not shrink from his duty. On 11 April, Truman announced that he had dismissed MacArthur. He noted that while debate is essential, 'military commanders must be governed by the policies and directives issued to them in the manner provided by our laws and Constitution.' MacArthur was unwilling to abide by the administration's policy, and thus had to be removed [Doc. 19].

The decision to adopt a limited war strategy in Korea was not popular, and public discontent focused on Truman's firing of MacArthur. Critics called for the president's removal from office (McCarthy told reporters 'The son of a bitch should be impeached'), and Congressional hearings were held [37 p. 359]. Truman's approval rating dropped below 30 percent, and would not rise higher than 33 percent for the remainder of his presidency. In the dispute, 69 percent sided with MacArthur, and telegrams to the White House ran 20–1 against Truman, some saying 'impeach the imbecile' and 'suggest you look for another Hiss in Blair House' (Truman's residence while the White House living quarters were being renovated) [103 p. 845]. MacArthur returned to the United States to a hero's welcome, including a ticker-tape parade and a speech before a joint session of Congress, in which he openly challenged the administration's Korea policy and declared famously, 'there is no substitute for victory' [*Doc. 20*]. But as that old soldier faded away, opinion on his dismissal began to change. The heads of the Joint Chiefs appeared before Congress and unanimously supported Truman's decision and Korea policy. In the words of Omar Bradley, to follow MacArthur's advice and take the war to China 'would involve us in the wrong war, at the wrong place, at the wrong time and with the wrong enemy' [*120 p. 232*].

With MacArthur on the sidelines, and the administration unanimous in support of a negotiated settlement, peace talks began in the spring of 1951. They would drag on for two bloody, inconclusive years, as both sides jockeyed for position along the front which roughly approximated the 38th parallel. The issue which caused the talks to stall was repatriation of prisoners of war. The communists insisted on the return of all of their troops, but many did not want to return. The Americans and South Koreans resisted sending back captured troops against their will. The stalemate over this issue would delay a cease-fire until July 1953, by which time Truman had left the White House and Stalin had died.

THE CONSEQUENCES OF KOREA

The Korean War marks an important turning point in the cold war. With the cold war in Europe largely static, it was a sign that future cold war conflicts were, ironically, more likely to take place in areas of less vital interest to the superpowers. With the exception of the second Berlin crisis of the late 1950s and early 1960s, each cold war hot spot would be outside Europe. With the interests of each side well-defined, neither challenged the position of the other, since that would surely mean war. But Europe was the only place with that clarity. The status of other areas was ambiguous at best. It is no mistake that the most costly cold war battles were fought outside Europe. In searching for advantage, both powers looked to areas where interests were not so clearly defined. The rest of the world was in flux, and thus the developing world in Asia, Africa and Latin America became the focus of future cold war battles. (The Korean War specifically contributed to the growing American attention to the communist threat in Asia, as US aid to the French increased in their war against the communist Viet Minh in Vietnam.)

Korea also established that it was no longer possible to fight total wars to unconditional surrender, since that threatened to lead to direct confrontation between the superpowers with unthinkable consequences. Thus future conflicts would, by necessity, be limited. Proxy wars, which did not directly involve both powers, were safer. Covert operations, in which the involvement of the superpower could remain at least plausibly deniable, could also avoid the problem of direct challenges to the interest of the other power, and the use of such operations would grow in the Eisenhower and Kennedy administrations.

NSC-68's argument that the United States would increasingly face an overt military challenge seemed validated by Korea, and the United States took an increasingly militarized approach to the cold war as a result. Aid to western Europe shifted to military purposes, defense spending increased dramatically. Greece and Turkey were added to NATO in 1951, American hostility toward Franco's Spain gave way to *rapprochement*, and the United States even reached a military co-operation agreement with the renegade communist state in Yugoslavia. In 1951 a formal peace treaty with Japan was signed, and the United States began showing greater concern for southeast Asia as the key to Japan's economic health. By 1953, US military production was seven times what it had been when the war began, and only a small part was going to Korea.

Korea also increased the power of the presidency within the American government. In the face of the North Korean attack, Truman ordered American forces into action on his authority as commander-in-chief. While he sought UN support, he did not request a declaration of war from Congress. Although American presidents had committed troops before without such an authorization, never had one done so on such a large scale for such an extended period of time. In bypassing Congress, Truman set the pattern for the rest of the cold war (and beyond). Millions of American troops have been deployed on numerous occasions and over 100,000 have died in combat, but the US Congress has not declared war since December 1941. Truman no doubt thought at first that explicit Congressional approval was unnecessary, given what he hoped would be the short duration of the action and the widespread, bipartisan support for his intervention. In the long run, however, it allowed critics to argue that it was Truman's, not America's, war, and his critics not unreasonably attributed the unpopular war to Truman alone.

Eventually, the unpopularity of the limited war which the United States fought in Korea contributed to the continuing collapse of bipartisanship in foreign policy. At an early stage in the war, Truman sought to recapture a sense of bipartisanship by calling out of retirement George Marshall, the symbol of his foreign policy successes of 1947–48. He asked Marshall to serve as Secretary of Defense. The reaction to the appointment was testimony to how much times had changed. Senator Taft and ten other Republicans voted against the nomination on the grounds that Marshall was responsible for losing China. Senator William Jenner called Marshall a 'living lie' and 'a front man for traitors' [113 *p. 197*]. By June 1951, McCarthy was openly charging that the architect of the American military victory in World War II was a traitor to his country, saying that as Secretary of State Marshall 'was implementing Stalin's will.' To remove any doubt, McCarthy added: 'I do not think that this monstrous perversion of sound and understandable national policy was accidental' [113 *pp. 199–200*]. Korea made a poisonous domestic atmosphere even worse.

CHAPTER TWELVE

'K$_1$C$_2$: KOREA, COMMUNISM AND CORRUPTION'

Whatever lingering hopes Harry Truman harbored for reviving the Fair Deal perished due to the victory of the CCP in China and the war in Korea. In his 1950 State of the Union address, Truman devoted most of his attention to foreign policy, but also included a series of domestic initiatives. When war broke out in Korea, at first liberals hoped that a swift and firm response there might immunize the administration against further red-baiting, but subsequent reversals in Korea produced the opposite effect. The initial rally-around-the-president phenomenon soon gave way to criticism of Truman's handling of the war. The fight in Korea would have been unnecessary, the China lobby argued, if Truman had prevented the triumph of Mao. By reversing course and adopting a more militant and military approach to the cold war, Truman implicitly agreed that his administration's policy before Korea had been inadequate. McCarthy claimed that the 'Korean deathtrap we can lay to the doors of the Kremlin and those who sabotaged rearming, including Acheson and the president' [37 p. 295].

DOMESTIC BACKLASH

Liberals were left demoralized by the Korean War. In the summer of 1950, Senator Pat McCarran of Nevada, the conservative Democratic counterpart to McCarthy, proposed the Internal Security Act of 1950, wedding the anxiety created by the Korean War to the fear of domestic communist subversion which had been growing since the end of World War II. The act called for the registration of all communists with the Justice Department, barred their employment by any branch of government, and prohibited entry into the United States to anyone advocating totalitarianism. On 22 September 1950, Truman vetoed the legislation as an unwarranted attack on civil liberties, a 'sedition bill' like the one used against the Jeffersonians in 1798. On this issue, Truman found himself increasingly isolated. Democrats deserted him, joining Republicans to override Truman's veto: only 48 members of the House and ten senators supported the president.

Although the intervention of the Chinese did not become apparent until after the 7 November Congressional elections, the Korean War had already changed the domestic political atmosphere. The arrest of Julius and Ethel Rosenberg, shortly after the outbreak of the Korean War, added to the growing fear of communists in the United States. The couple was charged with passing atomic secrets to the Soviets, and would later be executed by electric chair for treason [130]. In such an atmosphere, the outrageous charges of McCarthy gained more credibility, and soon 'McCarthyism' became a dominant campaign issue.

The leading Senate critic of McCarthy, Democratic Senator Millard Tydings of Maryland, was up for re-election. Tydings denounced McCarthy's charges of communists in government as a 'fraud' and a 'hoax,' marking him for special attention that fall by the senator from Wisconsin [113 p. 175]. McCarthy (who was not up for re-election, having been elected in 1946) made several trips into Maryland to campaign against Tydings. His Republican opponent used McCarthyite attacks in his campaign, including a doctored photograph purporting to show Tydings with the American Communist Party leader Earl Browder. Tydings went down to defeat, as did Scott Lucas of Illinois, the leader of the Senate Democrats, and Francis Myers of Pennsylvania, Senate Democratic whip.

In one of the most closely watched races, member of the House of Representatives Richard Nixon of California defeated the liberal Democrat Helen Gahagan Douglas in a scurrilous campaign which included a foretaste of the 'dirty tricks' which he would make famous a quarter-century later as president. Nixon called his opponent 'the Pink Lady' to imply that she had communist sympathies. (Her revenge was to call Nixon 'Tricky Dick,' a label that stuck.) Nixon charged his opponent with supporting 'the appeasing attitude of the State Department toward Communism,' and claimed that she followed the Communist Party line. His campaign sent out post-cards reading: 'Vote for Our Helen for Senator. We are with you 100%. The Communist League of Negro Women Voters' [116 pp. 210, 215]. Nixon won nearly 60 percent of the vote, attracting a number of traditionally Democratic voters. Nixon's campaign demonstrated the political power of red-baiting attacks in the 1950 elections.

Overall, the Democrats lost five Senate and 28 House seats, decreasing their majorities to two seats in the Senate and to 35 in the House. These losses, while substantial, were not unusual for the party in power in an off-year election (in fact, Truman pointed out at a press conference that it was the smallest loss by a party in power during an off-year election since the Wilson administration). There were of course other issues in these contests; for example, the oil industry in California opposed Douglas because of her opposition to the transfer of control of offshore oil from the federal to the state governments. Nonetheless, the election results were widely interpreted as a direct repudiation of Truman, and even the president himself privately had trouble seeing them as anything but a victory for McCarthyism.

The reversals in the Korean War due to the Chinese intervention further darkened the mood at the White House. Hopes for a cold war victory (and the resulting political boost at home) were dashed, and replaced by embarrassment and defeat. As American forces retreated in the face of the Chinese advance, the president was forced on 15 December 1950 to declare a state of national emergency and impose wage and price controls. In short, despite the initial talk of the military action in Korea as a limited 'police action,' the nation was put on a war footing, just five years after V-J day.

In such an atmosphere, Truman's domestic policy agenda was irrelevant. Diminished Democratic majorities in Congress, a war in Asia, and bitter partisan opposition at home made it impossible for Truman to do more than hold the line politically. Truman's January 1951 State of the Union address to Congress was his most conciliatory since 1947 (in the aftermath of the 1946 electoral débâcle). Truman focused almost entirely on foreign policy and war mobilization, downplaying the domestic agenda which he knew had no chance of passage. Much against his will, events had forced Truman to accept the conclusions of NSC-68: desirable domestic programs had to be shelved in the interest of a more assertive, military posture in the cold war. The actions of America's adversaries abroad and political realities at home dictated that outcome.

THE GROWING BURDEN

Overall, the burdens of the presidency began to weigh more heavily than ever on Truman. On 1 November 1950, two Puerto Rican nationalists attempted to assassinate Truman, killing one of his guards and wounding two others. The need to tighten security around the president limited his normal freedom of movement, particularly his daily morning walks. Truman lived in Blair House, across the street from the White House, while the living quarters were under renovation. Each morning, he later wrote in his dairy, 'I ride across the street in a car the roof of which will throw a grenade, the windows and sides turn a bullet and the floor will stop a land mine ... wonder why anyone would want to live like that' [5 p. 240]. Seven months after the attack, Truman had to turn down a social invitation in Missouri due to death threats. While expressing no concern for his own well-being, he told his cousin Ralph that 'what worries me is that some good fellow who has two or three kids may get killed – to keep me from that fate. You've no idea how it feels to have a grand man killed and two others badly wounded protecting you' [5 p. 212].

Truman became increasingly testy, his flashes of temper became more common. In early December 1950, the war was turning against the United States, and Truman's press secretary and old friend Charlie Ross died unexpectedly. It was at this time that Truman's most famous hastily-written letter became public. On the heels of these presidential and personal set-backs, Truman's daughter Margaret gave a concert performance in Washington, and received a rather harsh review from the music critic of the *Washington Post*. Truman, as he was sometimes wont to do, dashed off an angry letter, calling the critic 'a frustrated old man who wishes he could have been successful.' He went on to say that if they ever met, the critic would need 'a new nose, a lot of beefsteak for black eyes, and perhaps a supporter below!' Normally, Truman had the good sense not to send such intemperate letters, but not this time. One need not be a psychologist to see that the president was feeling the strain of his office, and his description of the critic might well indicate how Truman saw himself at that moment: 'a frustrated old man who wishes he could have been successful' [54 *p. 478*]. For all of his surface confidence, Truman harbored doubts about his ability to serve as president. In such dark moments as this, those fears got the better of him.

In the year that followed, the presidency continued to be a burden to Truman. He had often referred privately to the White House as the 'Great White Prison,' and it increasingly seemed that way to the beleaguered president. In addition to the fire storm created by his firing of MacArthur, Truman had to deal with growing accusations of corruption in his administration. The president's military aid, Harry Vaughan, was the target of many critics, particularly Arkansas Senator William Fulbright, who launched an investigation of various petty corruption charges in the spring of 1951. The Democratic senator first earned Truman's enmity in 1946, when in the aftermath of the elections he suggested that Truman appoint a Republican Secretary of State (then next in line to the presidency), and then resign. (Truman called him 'Half-bright,' a label Lyndon Johnson would later use when the Arkansan turned against the Vietnam War.) Fulbright aired charges of influence peddling at the Reconstruction Finance Corporation. The Securities and Exchange Commission, the Justice Department, and the Internal Revenue Service also came under scrutiny (the last leading to several resignations) [15; 40].

The president himself was scrupulously honest, but he seemed complacent, refusing to fire anyone, thus angering liberals along with his conservative critics. The accumulation of minor incidents created an aura of scandal around his administration. Truman was unfailingly loyal to his friends, even those who seemed to take advantage of his loyalty. In such cases, Truman seems to have placed his personal relations above political considerations. No doubt he recalled that his own career had been advanced by some less than reputable members of Tom Pendergast's Kansas City political machine. He saw his critics as hypocritical, often motivated by a McCarthyite desire to destroy his political friends. His refusal to sacrifice anyone on the altar of public opinion created the impression that nothing was being done about what critics called 'the mess in Washington.'

The ongoing stalemate in Korea continued to sap the president's public support. The inconclusive results of the peace talks convinced many Americans that MacArthur had been correct to oppose the administration's policy. By October 1951, a poll showed that 51 percent of the American people saw it as a 'useless war.' The war necessitated increased taxes along with wartime economic controls, further eroding public support. In Congress, Republican internationalism was weakened by the death of Senator Arthur Vandenberg, who worked so closely with the administration on aid to Greece and Turkey and the Marshall Plan. The GOP increasingly challenged the administration's focus on Europe, questioning the need to send more troops to reinforce NATO at a time when the Chinese communists were killing American troops in Korea. Former President Herbert Hoover even hinted at a new hemispheric isolationism.

THE 1952 CAMPAIGN

With the support of less than one-third of the public, an inconclusive war in Korea, diminishing clout with Congress, and feeling the weight of his office, Truman announced on 29 March 1952, that he would not be a candidate for re-election. Although the Twenty-second Amendment to the Constitution had been ratified in 1951 limiting future presidents to two terms (in reaction to FDR's record four elections), Truman was not affected by the amendment, and could have run for another term. Evidence suggests that he decided as early as the spring of 1950, that is, before the Korean War, not to run again. However, as late as 9 February 1952, he wrote in his diary that he was inclined to wait until the July convention to keep the nation in suspense, and then 'make the announcement as to whether I'll run or not.' That way, he felt, he could make a speech which the whole nation would watch, and he could 'nail the lies of the sabotage press and the lying air commentators and the columnists whose business it is to prostitute the minds of the voters' [5 *p. 238*]. Those remarks suggest that Truman was desperate to vindicate his record, and was still open to the possibility of running again. Certainly delaying an announcement until the convention would have made it virtually impossible for other candidates to line up support (that had been FDR's tactic in 1940).

In the end, after trying to interest several candidates in the nomination, Truman got behind the somewhat reluctant governor of Illinois, Adlai Stevenson [95; 104]. It was not so much that Stevenson was reluctant to be president, but that he did not want to be seen as Truman's hand-picked successor. With Truman's approval rating hovering around 30 percent, Stevenson did not want to associate himself too closely with the incumbent. When he publicly referred to the 'mess in Washington,' Truman was furious, seeing it as an act of political betrayal. The relationship between the president and the nominee was thus, to say the least, tense. Truman remained a loyal partisan, however, and campaigned strenuously for Stevenson and the entire Democratic ticket, no doubt hoping that a Democratic victory would be a vindication of sorts for his presidency.

That possibility grew more remote once the Republicans nominated General Dwight D. Eisenhower as their candidate. Ike, the commander of the D-Day invasion at Normandy in World War II, had been coveted by both parties since the end of the war. Truman even offered to support Eisenhower if he wanted to run on the Democratic ticket in 1948. Anti-Truman forces in the Democratic Party tried in vain to draft Eisenhower that same year. By avoiding involvement in either party in 1948, however, Eisenhower saved himself from being tainted by the results. He also added immeasurably to his basic appeal: the public saw him more than ever as a figure, like that other General-President, George Washington, who did not seek power. Ike thus came across as a unifier, someone above the partisan fray, not a power-hungry, scheming politician.

Those who knew Eisenhower had a somewhat different picture. Even during the war, General George S. Patton once observed that Eisenhower badly wanted to be president. And in fact, Ike's role in co-ordinating the Allied war effort in Europe was at least as political as it was military. He had to keep happy such diverse and larger-than-life personalities as Churchill, de Gaulle, FDR, Patton and the British Field Marshal Bernard L. Montgomery, which was no small political feat. To his admiring American public, however, Eisenhower remained a warm, sincere, reassuring authority figure.

After the shock of their defeat in 1948, the Republican Party was desperate for a guaranteed winner, and Eisenhower was high on the party's list. His only serious challenger for the nomination was Senator Robert Taft, son of the former president and head of the isolationist wing of the Republican Party. As head of NATO in 1951, Eisenhower was disappointed in the lack of support for the alliance he saw in Taft and other Republicans, and became convinced of the need to turn the GOP toward internationalism. Other Republican internationalists, like the 1948 nominee Thomas Dewey, and Massachusetts Senator Henry Cabot Lodge, urged Eisenhower to run, telling him that the country needed him to save it from New Deal big government on the one hand and isolationism on the other. When he won the 1952 New Hampshire primary without even being an announced candidate, Eisenhower resigned his position with NATO, and returned to the United States to become formally a candidate for president [115].

Eisenhower soon revealed himself as a conservative devoted to a limited federal government, but he avoided the extreme wing of the party which wanted to roll back the New Deal. He recognized that the social safety net established by the Social Security Act commanded widespread public support, and that it was political suicide to oppose it. Just as he hoped to lead the Republicans from their dangerous flirtation with isolationism, he also wanted to adjust its domestic agenda to one of limiting, not undoing, the New Deal.

In a campaign speech in Boise, Idaho in August 1952, Eisenhower spoke of a 'middle way' in American politics. He took it for granted that 'all Americans of all parties have now accepted and will forever support what we call social gains, the security that people are entitled to in their old age and to make certain they are adequately cared for, insurance against unemployment, equal opportunities.' However, he also criticized the New Deal philosophy in which 'Government does everything but come and wash the dishes for the housewife' and whose 'answer to evils in Government is more Government' [*Doc. 21*].

Ike's 'modern Republicanism'* blended an acceptance of the permanence of the New Deal's limited welfare state with a Herbert Hoover-style individualism, self-reliance and business–government co-operation. The reforms of the 1930s were, Eisenhower said, 'a solid floor that keeps all of us from falling into the pit of disaster.' But he added, appealing to traditional Republican ideals, 'on top of that floor, let's not interfere with the incentive, the ambition, the right of any of you to build the most glorious structure on top of that floor that you can imagine.' While the Republican right wing was critical of his acceptance of the New Deal's social safety net, his appeal with the mainstream voter only grew [*Doc. 21*].

In the end, the Republican convention chose Ike over Taft for one simple reason: Eisenhower was a sure winner, and the party had lost five consecutive presidential elections, the longest losing streak of a major party in American history. Eisenhower held the promise of attracting many independent voters who had been siding with the Democrats since the Depression. He was the candidate who represented the broad middle in American politics: internationalist in foreign policy (but in no way tainted by Yalta, China or Korea) and fiscally conservative in a time of growing prosperity (but not hostile to the entitlements and security to which middle-class Americans had become accustomed). In an ironic twist, the Republican candidate in 1952 reflected the historic successes of the Democratic Truman administration: the marginalization of isolationism in foreign policy and the institutionalization of the New Deal in domestic affairs.

To be sure, Ike attacked the record of the Democrats in many ways. The Republican campaign formula was 'K$_1$C$_2$: Korea, Communism and Corruption,' the three weak points of the Truman administration. Ike's choice of the young Richard Nixon as his running mate symbolized those partisan differences. Nixon was a vociferous anti-communist and a tireless critic of the Truman administration, and he gladly took on the role of partisan battler while Ike tried to remain above it all. In one of his more famous rhetorical excesses, Nixon said that the Democratic nominee Adlai Stevenson 'holds a Ph.D. from Acheson's College of Cowardly Communist Containment' [116 *p. 228*].

Nixon's comment indicates one of the campaign themes of the Republican campaign in 1952. Not about to make the same mistake as in 1948, they made foreign policy, containment in particular, an issue. The ticket criticized containment as too defensive, and began talking of 'rollback' and 'liberation' in the Eisenhower administration, tapping into the sentiment which led so many Americans to support MacArthur. Without being specific about his plans, Eisenhower announced that if elected, 'I will go to Korea,' implying that he would break the stalemate which stumped Truman. Ike promised a government which 'does not grow complacent, that does not grow away from the people and become indifferent to them, that does not become arrogant in the exercise of its powers' [*Doc. 21*]. He pledged to return morality to a capitol corrupted and infiltrated by communists during 20 uninterrupted years of Democratic rule, and fiscal responsibility and sound business principles to a government which had grown unimaginably large since the last Republican presidency.

The result was a personal triumph. Eisenhower out-polled Stevenson by over six million votes, and won an electoral college landslide, 442–89. He lost only nine states, and even won four southern states in the usually solid Democratic south. Eisenhower campaigned in the south, and his success there was another sign of things to come, a crack in the traditional Democratic dominance of the region (due in part to Truman's embrace of civil rights) which his running mate would later exploit in his own successful presidential campaign in 1968. Eisenhower's presence on the ticket also helped Republicans to regain narrow control of both houses of Congress (48–47 in the Senate, 221–214 in the House). Washington was once again a Republican city.

CHAPTER THIRTEEN

CONCLUSION

THE END OF AN ERA

In a larger sense, however, it was still the city of Franklin D. Roosevelt and Harry S. Truman. Ike could not win by campaigning against the New Deal and did not try. Despite his rhetorical challenge to the administration's foreign policy, he remained firmly in the tradition of the Eurocentric internationalism of FDR and Truman. The way in which he won the election of 1952 was actually an affirmation of the basic accomplishments of the Truman administration, though it was a repudiation of certain surface aspects of recent years – it was an attack on immediate issues such as the inconclusive Korean War, internal security, and petty corruption, none of which truly went to fundamental principles.

The Eisenhower administration would quickly dispatch these issues. The death of Stalin in March 1953 opened up the possibility of a new US–Soviet relationship and an end to the war in Korea, and a cease-fire was reached in July 1953. While McCarthy continued his crusade against communists in government, other Republicans lost interest in the issue now that the government was controlled by the GOP. Eisenhower worked behind the scenes to undermine McCarthy (although he accepted his support in the 1952 campaign), and when the senator from Wisconsin overreached in the Army–McCarthy hearings in 1954, Eisenhower assisted in his downfall. The replacement of longtime Democratic office holders neutralized charges of executive branch corruption.

On the important issues of the day, however, the legacy of the Truman administration was clear. For all the talk of liberation and rollback, the Eisenhower administration's foreign policy was merely a different strategy of containment, to use the phrase of an eminent cold war historian, not a repudiation of Truman's policy [48]. When opportunities arose to pursue rollback, such as when East Germans rebelled against communist rule in 1953 and the Hungarians started an anti-communist revolution in 1956, Eisenhower prudently avoided interference, and watched the Soviets re-establish control in both countries. The *status quo* in Europe, which the

100

Truman administration accepted, was maintained by its successors. All subsequent presidents recognized that it was simply too dangerous to challenge the Soviet position in eastern Europe. Even when the communist regimes there collapsed in 1989, it was the policy of the Bush administration to keep quiet and avoid even the appearance of gloating. Any sense that the United States was seeking to take advantage of the situation threatened to provoke the Soviets into cracking down rather than letting go.

The Eisenhower administration did seek to make the cold war cheaper to prosecute by shifting to the doctrine of massive retaliation, which sought to prevent future Koreas by warning the Soviets that aggression might well be met not with a proportionate conventional response but with overwhelming nuclear retaliation. Eisenhower thus sought to keep defense spending under control, by relying more on relatively inexpensive nuclear weapons rather that the large conventional forces envisioned by NSC-68. Nonetheless, the goal was the same: to prevent the spread of Soviet power and communist ideology. When the Kennedy administration took over in 1961, it returned to an emphasis on greater defense spending (both nuclear and conventional) and a dedication to aggressively waging the cold war.

For better or worse, the United States continued to view the world in terms defined by the Truman administration, seeing the Soviet Union and its ideology as mortal threats to the United States which must be opposed all around the world. The persistence of this world-view is nowhere more apparent than in the American intervention in Vietnam. It was the mind set of the Truman administration which ultimately led to that tragic and misguided war. Although George Kennan never envisioned a containment policy which was primarily military or universal in its application, it soon took that form, due in large part to the Korean War. The very success of containment in Europe, American leaders came to believe, had caused the Soviets to adopt a more overtly military strategy, and to seek opportunities in other areas of the world. Just as the United States had responded in Europe, the logic ran, it must respond elsewhere as well.

Universalist tendencies in American thought then took over: even if Korea itself were not crucial to American security, failure to respond in that situation could signal a lack of resolve, and undermine American credibility in other, more crucial areas such as western Europe. Thus the distinction between peripheral and vital interests dissolved, since the failure to defend even peripheral interests might weaken the ability to defend vital ones.

The American economic world-view also dovetailed nicely into this perspective. If American security was dependent on domestic prosperity, and that prosperity required the maximization of world trade, the progressive loss of nations to the communist bloc could, in the long run, erode the foundation of American economic health by denying the United States and its allies access to raw materials and foreign markets. Thus it became even more important to draw and hold the line against the spread of communist ideology, wherever it might appear.

These ideas were bequeathed to Truman's successors, and applied to the unlikely nation of Vietnam. Four presidents, two from each major political party, never seriously questioned the need to follow these basic precepts. Consequently, the United States committed itself incrementally to preventing a communist victory in Vietnam, until it became a national nightmare which played a role in the destruction of two presidencies, and led the nation to doubt its strength, its wisdom, and for some, even its morality.

The long-term evaluation of the Truman foreign policy is therefore decidedly mixed. In the end, its containment policy had the effect which Kennan foresaw in the mid-1940s: the slow, gradual mellowing of the Soviet regime, followed by its collapse. It took far longer than Kennan expected, and the patience of the American people was sorely taxed in the process, but it worked: the contest ended favorably for the United States, without the two superpowers ever going to war with each other.

On the other hand, the cost was tremendous. US domestic needs during the cold war often took a back seat to the presumed imperative of meeting the Soviet threat. On at least one occasion, the Cuban missile crisis, the cold war came frighteningly close to an all-out nuclear war which might have ended civilization. In many instances, Vietnam being only the most costly for Americans, the relentless dedication to containment led to numerous smaller 'hot' wars which left millions of people dead. Whatever one's ultimate judgement, however, one thing is clear: the basic outlines of the cold war were set during the Truman years.

Domestically, the story is the same. Politically, postwar debates about the size and role of the federal government are still conducted in the terms set during Truman's presidency: Democrats are more likely to favor policies which require that the federal government play a large part, while Republicans favor a more limited role. Even more significantly, however, neither party argues that the federal government is not responsible for the management of the economy and the minimal economic well-being of Americans, a function which became institutionalized under Truman.

The lack of dramatic shift in the transition from Truman to Eisenhower makes this point. While Eisenhower brought more fiscal discipline to the federal budget, much of the restraint came in the defense budget which Truman tried and ultimately failed to keep low. Ike's focus on balancing the budget marked a return to Republican economic orthodoxy, but when recession came (as it did several times during his two terms), New Deal reforms such as unemployment insurance automatically kicked in and helped to prevent a repeat of the economic calamity of the 1930s. Eisenhower resisted any great expansion of the role of the federal government, but worked well with the Democratic leadership in Congress after they regained control of both Houses in the 1954 elections and forged consensus policies which reflected the relatively small differences between the two parties.

When Democrats regained control of the White House in the 1960s, both John Kennedy and Lyndon Johnson reached back to the unfulfilled program of Harry Truman. JFK's 'New Frontier' was little more than a re-packaging of the Fair Deal. LBJ's 'Great Society' was more ambitious, but it too drew from ideas presented earlier by Truman, such as national health insurance. In 1965, when Congress passed the bill establishing Medicare and Medicaid (health insurance for the elderly and the poor), Johnson even paid tribute to his predecessor by traveling to Independence, Missouri and signing them into law in the presence of Truman. In the 1990s, the question of the proper role of the federal government in ensuring health care for all its citizens remained one of the most controversial topics in American politics. Similarly, as budget deficits gave way to budget surpluses in the late 1990s, the debate over tax cuts echoed the rhetoric of the Truman years: Truman's explanation of his veto in 1947 [*Doc. 9*] might have been easily repeated by President Clinton in 1999.

Socially, the United States in the late twentieth century would likely be unrecognizable to Harry Truman and his generation. Yet the changes to come all had precedents during the formative postwar years. After the emergency of the war ended, most women returned to the home from the factory. But throughout the late 1940s and early 1950s, women gradually returned to the workplace, not so much out of national need as for their own personal reasons. The social convention that men worked while women stayed at home began to erode.

African-Americans after the war also seized new opportunities. More than ever before, they began to challenge the United States to live up to its best ideals and reject its basest fears. Through judicial challenges, political action and grassroots organizing, they made it clear that a prejudiced, segregationist *status quo* was not acceptable. In that struggle, they found an unlikely ally in Harry Truman, who alienated the Democratic Party's southern wing in a way FDR never dared, and made civil rights a permanent part of the Democratic reform program.

The Truman years set the pattern for the political, economic, social and diplomatic trends which would mark the United States for the remainder of the twentieth century. Most significantly, they saw the institutionalization of the limited welfare state established by the New Deal, and the creation of an internationalist foreign policy and attitude of world leadership which would outlast their immediate cause, the cold war with the Soviet Union. Improbably presiding over it all was the man from Independence, Harry S. Truman, a man of the nineteenth century whose presidency shaped his nation for most of the twentieth century.

When he left Washington on 20 January 1953, Harry Truman did not enjoy the widespread admiration of his fellow Americans. Upon his arrival at his home in Missouri, he found that thousands had come out to welcome him: 'It was the pay-off for thirty years of hell and hard work,' he wrote in his diary [5 *p. 288*]. In the decades since, Truman has received a different 'pay-off': his reputation has improved markedly, and historians generally rank him among the 'near-great' presidents. While many are still critical of various aspects of his presidency, few argue that it lacked lasting significance.

Several days after he became president, Truman set down this account of the day.

I arrived at [Speaker of the House Sam] Rayburn's office about 5:05 and there was a call from [FDR's press secretary] Steve Early asking me to come to the White House as quickly as possible … arrived there about 5:25 p.m., I should say, and was ushered into Mrs. Roosevelt's study on second floor. …

Mrs. Roosevelt put her arm around my shoulder and said, 'The President is dead.' That was the first inkling I had of the seriousness of the situation.

I then asked them what I could do, and she said – 'What can we do for you?' Before I had a chance to answer her question, Secretary of State Stettinius came in. He evidently had received the news because he was in tears. …

They left about a half an hour after the Cabinet meeting adjourned I should say, and I went on home to my apartment at 4701 Connecticut Avenue.

I was very much shocked. I am not easily shocked but was certainly shocked when I was told of the President's death and the weight of the Government had fallen on my shoulders. I did not know what reaction the country would have to the death of a man whom they all practically worshipped. I was worried about the reaction of the Armed Forces. I did not know what effect the situation would have on the war effort, price control, war production and everything that entered into the emergency that then existed. I knew the President had a great many meetings with Churchill and Stalin. I was not familiar with any of these things and it was really something to think about but I decided the best thing to do was to go home and get as much rest as possible and face the music.

My wife and daughter and mother-in-law were at the apartment of our next door neighbor, and their daughter Mrs. Irving Wright was present. They had a turkey dinner and they gave us something to eat. I had not had anything to eat since noon. Went to bed, went to sleep, and did not worry any more.

Ferrell, [5], pp. 14–16.

DOCUMENT 2   HARRY S. TRUMAN, STATEMENT ANNOUNCING THE
USE OF THE A-BOMB AT HIROSHIMA, 6 AUGUST 1945

The president's statement to the public reporting the use of the atomic bomb.

Sixteen hours ago an American airplane dropped one bomb on Hiroshima, an important Japanese Army base. That bomb had more power than 20,000 tons of T.N.T. It had more than two thousand times the blast power of the British 'Grand Slam' which is the largest bomb ever yet used in the history of warfare.

The Japanese began the war from the air at Pearl Harbor. They have been repaid many fold. And the end is not yet. With this bomb we have now added a new and revolutionary increase in destruction to supplement the growing power of our armed forces. In their present form these bombs are now in production and even more powerful forms are in development.

It is an atomic bomb. It is the harnessing of the basic power of the universe. The force from which the sun draws its power has been loosed against those who brought the war to the Far East. ...

The battle of the laboratories held fateful risks for us as well as the battles of the air, land and sea, and we have now won the battle of the laboratories as we have won the other battles. ...

We are now prepared to obliterate more rapidly and completely every productive enterprise the Japanese have above ground in any city. We shall destroy their docks, their factories, and their communications. Let there be no mistake; we shall completely destroy Japan's power to make war.

It was to spare the Japanese people from utter destruction that the ultimatum of July 26 was issued at Potsdam. Their leaders promptly rejected that ultimatum. If they do not now accept our terms they may expect a rain of ruin from the air, the like of which has never been seen on this earth. Behind this attack will follow land and sea forces in such numbers and power as they have not seen and with the fighting skill of which they are already well aware. ...

The fact that we can release atomic energy ushers in a new era in man's understanding of nature's forces. ... I shall recommend that the Congress of the United States consider promptly the establishment of an appropriate commission to control the production and use of atomic power within the United States. I shall give further consideration and make further recommendations to the Congress as to how atomic power can become a powerful and forceful influence towards the maintenance of world peace.

Public Papers of the President, Harry S. Truman, 1945, [7], pp. 197–200.

*In this address to Congress, Truman attempts to revive the New Deal and
FDR's Economic Bill of Rights, clearly revealing his liberalism.*

The Congress convenes at a time of great emergency. It is an emergency
about which, however, we need have no undue fear if we exercise the same
energy, foresight, and wisdom as we did in carrying on the war and winning
this victory. ...

The process of reconversion will be a complicated and difficult one. The
general line of approach to the problem is to achieve as full peacetime
production and employment as possible in the most efficient and speedy
manner. The following policies have been laid down and will be followed:

(1) Demobilize as soon as possible the armed forces no longer needed.
(2) Cancel and settle war contracts as quickly as possible.
(3) Clear the war plants so as to permit contractors to proceed with
     peacetime production.
(4) Hold the line on prices and rents until fair competition can operate to
     prevent inflation and undue hardship on consumers.
(5) Hold wages in line where their increase would cause inflationary price
     rises. Where prices would not be endangered, collective bargaining
     should be restored.
(6) Remove all possible wartime government controls in order to speed and
     encourage reconversion and expansion.
(7) Keep only those controls which are necessary to help reconversion and
     expansion by preventing bottlenecks, shortages of material, and
     inflation.
(8) Prevent rapid decrease of wage incomes or purchasing power.
     The major objective, of course, is to reestablish an expanded peacetime
     industry, trade, and agriculture, and to do it as quickly as possible.

Obviously during this process there will be a great deal of inevitable
unemployment. What we must do is to assist industry to reconvert to peacetime production as quickly and as effectively as possible so that the number
of unemployed will be swiftly and substantially reduced as industry and
business and agriculture get into high production. ...

Obviously, displaced war workers cannot find jobs until industry has
been regeared and made ready to produce peacetime goods. During this lag
the Government should provide help. The cost of this transition from war to
peace is as much a part of the cost of war as the transition from peace to war
– and we should so consider it. ...

The foundations of a healthy economy cannot be secure so long as any large section of our working people receive substandard wages. The existence of substandard wage levels sharply curtails the national purchasing power and narrows the market for the products of our farms and factories. ...

I believed that the goal of a 40 cent minimum was inadequate when established [in 1938]. It has now become obsolete. ... I therefore recommend that the Congress amend the Fair Labor Standards Act by substantially increasing the minimum wage specified therein to a level which will eliminate substandards of living, and assure the maintenance of the health, efficiency and general well-being of workers. ...

The American people have set high goals for their own future. They have set these goals high because they have seen how great can be the productive capacity of our country. The levels of production and income reached during the war years have given our citizens an appreciation of what a full production peacetime economy can be.

They are not interested in boom prosperity – for that only too often leads to panic and depression. But they are interested in providing opportunity for work and for ultimate security. Government must do its part and assist industry and labor to get over the line from war to peace.

That is why I have asked for unemployment compensation legislation.

That is why I now ask for full-employment legislation.

The objectives for our domestic economy which we seek in our long-range plans were summarized by the late President Franklin D. Roosevelt over a year and a half ago in the form of an economic bill of rights. Let us make the attainment of those rights the essence of postwar American economic life. ...

A national reassertion of the right to work for every American citizen able and willing to work – a declaration of the ultimate duty of Government to use its own resources if all other methods should fail to prevent prolonged unemployment – these will help to avert fear and establish full employment. The prompt and firm acceptance of this bedrock public responsibility will reduce the need for its exercise. I ask that full-employment legislation to provide these vital assurances be speedily enacted. ...

During the years of war production we made substantial progress in overcoming many of the prejudices which had resulted in discrimination against minority groups. ... In the reconversion period and thereafter, we should make every effort to continue this American ideal. ... I have already requested that legislation be enacted placing the Fair Employment Practice Committee on a permanent basis. I repeat that recommendation. ...

Those who have the responsibility of labor relations must recognize that responsibility. This is not the time for short-sighted management to seize upon the chance to reduce wages and try to injure labor unions. Equally it is not the time for labor leaders to shirk their responsibility and permit widespread industrial strife. ...

After the First World War farm prices dropped more than 50 percent from the spring of 1920 to the spring of 1921. We do not intend to permit a repetition of the disaster that followed the First World War. The Secretary of Agriculture has assured me that he will use all means now authorized by the Congress to carry out the price-support commitments. ...

The present shortage of decent homes and the enforced widespread use of substandard housing indicate vital unfilled needs of the Nation. These needs will become more marked as veterans begin to come back and look for places to live. ... I urgently recommend that the Congress, at an early date, enact broad and comprehensive housing legislation. ...

I shall shortly communicate with the Congress recommending a national health program to provide adequate medical care for all Americans and to protect them from financial loss and hardships resulting from illness and accident. I shall also communicate with the Congress with respect to expanding our social-security system, and improving our program of education for our citizens.

In this hour of victory over our enemies abroad, let us now resolve to use all of our efforts and energies to build a better life here at home and a better world for generations to come.

Public Papers of the President, Harry S. Truman, 1945, [7], pp. 264–309.

DOCUMENT 4	HARRY S. TRUMAN, STATEMENT UPON SIGNING THE EMPLOYMENT ACT, 20 FEBRUARY 1946

Truman expresses the liberal belief in government's responsibility to manage the economy and provide jobs for Americans.

I have signed today the Employment Act of 1946. In enacting this legislation the Congress and the President are responding to an overwhelming demand of the people. The legislation gives expression to a deep-seated desire for a conscious and positive attack upon the ever-recurring problems of mass unemployment and ruinous depression. ...

Democratic government has the responsibility to use all its resources to create and maintain conditions under which free enterprise can operate efficiently. ... It is not the Government's duty to supplant the efforts of private enterprise to find markets, or of individuals to find jobs. The people do expect the Government, however, to create and maintain conditions in which the individual businessman and the individual job seeker have a chance to succeed by their own efforts. That is the objective of the Employment Act of 1946. ...

The result is not all that I had hoped for, but ... [t]he Employment Act of 1946 is not the end of a road, but rather the beginning. It is a commitment by the Government to the people – a commitment to take any and all measures necessary for a healthy economy, one that provides opportunities for those able, willing and seeking to work.

Public Papers of the President, Harry S. Truman, 1946, [7], pp. 125–6.

DOCUMENT 5   GEORGE F. KENNAN, 'THE LONG TELEGRAM,'
22 FEBRUARY 1946

An influential message which expresses what would become the containment policy toward the Soviet Union, by the long-time State Department expert on Russia and the Soviet Union (at the time stationed at the US Embassy in Moscow).

At bottom of Kremlin's neurotic view of world affairs is traditional and instinctive Russian sense of insecurity. ... They have always feared foreign penetration, feared direct contact between Western world and their own, feared what would happen if Russians learned truth about world without it or if foreigners learned truth about world within. And they learned to seek security only in patient but deadly struggle for total destruction of rival power, never in compacts and compromises with it. ...

Basically this is only the steady advance of uneasy Russian nationalism, a centuries old movement in which conceptions of offense and defense are inextricably confused. But in new guise of international Marxism, with its honeyed promises to a desperate and war torn outside world, it is more dangerous and insidious than ever before. ...

In summary, we have here a political force committed fanatically to the belief that with US there can be no permanent modus vivendi, that it is desirable and necessary that the internal harmony of our society be disrupted, our traditional way of life be destroyed, the international authority of our state be broken, if Soviet power is to be secure. ... This is admittedly not a pretty picture. Problem of how to cope with this force [is] undoubtedly greatest task our diplomacy has ever faced and probably greatest it will ever have to face. It should be point of departure from which our political general staff work at present should proceed. It should be approached with same thoroughness and care as solution of major strategic problem in war, and if necessary, with no smaller outlay in planning effort. I cannot attempt to suggest all answers here. But I would like to record my conviction that problem is within our power to solve – and that without recourse to any general military conflict.

US Department of State, *Foreign Relations of the United States, 1946,* Vol. VI, *Eastern Europe; the Soviet Union,* [12], pp. 696–709.

In one of the most important addresses of the emerging cold war, the former British prime minister and wartime leader warns Americans of the new threat posed by the Soviet Union.

The United States stands at this time at the pinnacle of world power. It is a solemn moment for the American democracy. With primacy in power is also joined an awe-inspiring accountability to the future. As you look around you, you feel not only the sense of duty done but also feel anxiety lest you fall below the level of achievement. Opportunity is here now, clear and shining, for both our countries. To reject it or ignore it or fritter it away will bring upon us all the long reproaches of the after-time. It is necessary that constancy of mind, persistency of purpose, and the grand simplicity of decision shall guide and rule the conduct of the English-speaking peoples in peace as they did in war. ...

A shadow has fallen upon the scenes so lately lighted by the Allied victory. Nobody knows what Soviet Russia and its Communist international organization intends to do in the immediate future, or what are the limits, if any, to their expansive and proselytizing tendencies. ... We understand the Russian need to be secure on her western frontiers from all renewal of German aggression. We welcome her to her rightful place among the leading nations of the world. Above all, we welcome constant, frequent, and growing contacts between Russian people and our own people on both sides of the Atlantic. It is my duty, however, to place before you certain facts about the present position in Europe.

From Stettin in the Baltic to Trieste in the Adriatic, an iron curtain has descended across the continent. Behind it lie all the capitals of the ancient states of Central and Eastern Europe. Warsaw, Berlin, Prague, Vienna, Budapest, Belgrade, Bucharest, and Sofia, all these famous cities and the populations around them lie in the Soviet sphere and all are subject, in one form or another, not only to Soviet influence but to a very high and increasing measure of control from Moscow. Athens alone, with its immortal glories, is free to decide its future at an election under British, American and French observation. ...

The Communist parties, which were very small in all these eastern states of Europe, have been raised to preeminence and power far beyond their numbers and are seeking everywhere to obtain totalitarian control. Police governments are prevailing in nearly every case, and so far, except in Czechoslovakia, there is no true democracy. ... Whatever conclusions may be drawn from these facts – and facts they are – this is certainly not the liberated Europe we fought to build up. Nor is it one which contains the essentials of permanent peace. ...

Our difficulties and dangers will not be removed by closing our eyes to them; they will not be removed by mere waiting to see what happens; nor will they be relieved by a policy of appeasement. ... From what I have seen of our Russian friends and allies during the war, I am convinced that there is nothing they admire as much as strength, and there is nothing for which they have less respect than for military weakness. For that reason the old doctrine of a balance of power is unsound. We cannot afford, if we can help it, to work on narrow margins, offering temptations to a trial of strength. If the Western democracies stand together in strict adherence to the principles of the United Nations Charter, their influence for furthering those principles will be immense and no one is likely to molest them. If, however, they become divided or falter in their duty, and if these all-important years are allowed to slip away, then indeed catastrophe may overwhelm us all.

Reprinted in Judge, [6], pp. 15–17.

DOCUMENT 7	HENRY A. WALLACE, LETTER TO PRESIDENT TRUMAN, 23 JULY 1946

The former vice-president and most liberal member of Truman's cabinet challenges the direction of administration foreign policy.

I have been increasingly concerned about the trend of international affairs since the end of the war, and I am even more troubled by the apparently growing feeling among the American people that another war is coming and the only way that we can head it off is to arm ourselves to the teeth. Yet all of past history indicates that an armaments race does not lead to peace but to war. The months just ahead may well be the crucial period which will decide whether the civilized world will go down in destruction after the five or ten years needed for several nations to arm themselves with atomic bombs. Therefore, I want to give you my views on how the present trend toward conflict might be averted. ...

How do American actions since V-J Day appear to other nations? I mean by actions concrete things like the $13 billion for the War and Navy Departments, the Bikini tests of the atomic bomb and continued production of bombs, the plan to arm Latin America with our weapons, production of B-29s and planned production of B-36s, and the effort to secure air bases spread over half the globe from which the other half of the globe can be bombed. I cannot but feel that these actions must make it look to the rest of the world as if we were only paying lip service to peace.

These facts rather make it appear either (1) that we are preparing ourselves to win the war which we regard as inevitable or (2) that we are trying to build up predominance of force to intimidate the rest of mankind. How would it look to us if Russia had the atomic bomb and we did not, if Russia had 10,000-mile bombers and air bases within a thousand miles of our coastlines, and we did not? ...

Our basic mistrust of the Russians, which has been greatly intensified in recent months by the playing up of conflict in the press, stems from differences in political and economic organization. For the first time in our history defeatists among us have raised the fear of another system as a successful rival to democracy and free enterprise in other countries and perhaps even our own. I am convinced that we can meet that challenge as we have in the past by demonstrating that economic abundance can be achieved without sacrificing personal, political and religious liberties. We cannot meet it as Hitler tried to by an anti-Comintern alliance. ...

We should make an effort to counteract the irrational fear of Russia which is being systematically built up in the American people by certain individuals and publications. ... We should not act as if we too felt that we were threatened in today's world. We are by far the most powerful nation in the world, the only allied nation which came out of the war without devastation and much stronger than before the war. Any talk on our part about the need for strengthening our defenses further is bound to appear hypocritical to other nations.

Harry Truman Papers, Harry S. Truman Library, Independence, MO, reprinted in Chafe, [31], pp. 34–9.

DOCUMENT 8   HARRY S. TRUMAN, ADDRESS TO THE US CONGRESS, 12 MARCH 1947

The president's statement of what became known as the Truman Doctrine is often considered the American declaration of the cold war, and established the policy of containment which would guide American foreign policy for 40 years.

I am fully aware of the broad implications involved if the United States extends assistance to Greece and Turkey, and I shall discuss these implications with you at this time.

One of the primary objectives of the foreign policy of the United States is the creation of conditions in which we and other nations will be able to work out a way of life free from coercion. This was a fundamental issue in the war with Germany and Japan. Our victory was won over countries which sought to impose their will, and their way of life, upon other nations.

To ensure the peaceful development of nations, free from coercion, the United States has taken a leading part in establishing the United Nations. The United Nations is designed to make possible lasting freedom and independence for all its members. We shall not realize our objectives, however, unless we are willing to help free peoples to maintain their free institutions and their national integrity against aggressive movements that seek to impose upon them totalitarian regimes. This is no more than a frank recognition that totalitarian regimes imposed upon free peoples, by direct or indirect aggression, undermine the foundations of international peace and hence the security of the United States.

The peoples of a number of countries in the world have recently had totalitarian regimes forced upon them against their will. The Government of the United States has made frequent protests against coercion and intimidation, in violation of the Yalta agreement, in Poland, Rumania, and Bulgaria. I must also state that in a number of other countries there have been similar developments.

At the present moment in world history nearly every nation must choose between alternative ways of life. The choice is too often not a free one.

One way of life is based upon the will of the majority, and is distinguished by free institutions, representative government, free elections, guarantees of individual liberty, freedom of speech and religion, and freedom from political oppression.

The second way of life is based upon the will of a minority forcibly imposed upon the majority. It relies upon terror and oppression, a controlled press and radio, fixed elections, and the suppression of personal freedoms.

I believe it must be the policy of the United States to support free peoples who are resisting attempted subjugation by armed minorities or by outside pressures.

I believe that we must assist free peoples to work out their own destinies in their own way.

I believe that our help should be primarily through economic and financial aid which is essential to economic stability and orderly political processes. ...

It would be an unspeakable tragedy if [Greece and Turkey], which have struggled so long against overwhelming odds, should lose that victory for which they have sacrificed so much. Collapse of free institutions and loss of independence would be disastrous not only for them but for the world. Discouragement and possibly failure would quickly be the lot of neighboring peoples striving to maintain their freedom and independence. ...

This is a serious course upon which we embark.

I would not recommend it except that the alternative is much more serious. The United States contributed $341,000,000,000 toward winning World War II. This is an investment in world freedom and world peace.

The assistance that I am recommending for Greece and Turkey amounts to little more than 1/10 of 1 percent of this investment. It is only common sense that we should safeguard this investment and make sure that it was not in vain.

The seeds of totalitarian regimes are nurtured by misery and want. They spread and grow in the evil soil of poverty and strife. They reach their full growth when the hope of a people for a better life has died.

We must keep that hope alive.

The free peoples of the world look to us for support in maintaining their freedoms.

If we falter in our leadership, we may endanger the peace of the world – and we shall surely endanger the welfare of this Nation.

Great responsibilities have been placed upon us by the swift movement of events. I am confident that the Congress will face these responsibilities squarely.

Public Papers of the President, Harry S. Truman, 1947, [7], pp. 176–80.

DOCUMENT 9   **HARRY S. TRUMAN, VETO OF BILL TO REDUCE INCOME TAXES, 16 JUNE 1947**

An example of Truman's confrontational policy toward the Republican 80th Congress, portraying the Republicans as favoring the wealthy, while the president protects the lower classes.

I have reached the conclusion that this bill represents the wrong kind of tax reduction, at the wrong time. It offers dubious, ill-apportioned, and risky benefits at the expense of a sound tax policy and is, from the standpoint of Government finances, unsafe. ...

With the present huge public debt, it is of first importance that every effort now be made to reduce the debt as much as possible. ... In addition to the fact that this is not the time for tax reduction, there is a fundamental objection to this particular bill. An adjustment of the tax system should provide fair and equitable relief for individuals. ... A good tax bill would give a greater proportion of relief to the low income group.

Public Papers of the President, Harry S. Truman, 1947, [7], p. 281.

DOCUMENT 10   **HARRY S. TRUMAN, RADIO ADDRESS TO THE AMERICAN PEOPLE ON THE VETO OF THE TAFT–HARTLEY BILL, 20 JUNE 1947**

The president denounces the bill as an attack on labor and begins to rebuild his damaged relationship with American unions.

At noon today I sent to Congress a message vetoing the Taft–Hartley bill. I vetoed this bill because I am convinced it is a bad bill. It is bad for labor, bad for management, and bad for the country.

I had hoped that the Congress would send me a labor bill I could sign.

I have said before, and I say it now, that we need legislation to correct abuses in the field of labor relations. ... But the Taft–Hartley bill is a shocking piece of legislation. It is unfair to the working people of this country. ... Under no circumstances could I have signed *this* bill! ...

It would take us back in the direction of individual bargaining. It would take the bargaining power away from the workers and give more power to management. This bill would even take away from our workingmen some bargaining rights which they enjoyed before the Wagner Act was passed 12 years ago. ...

As our generous American spirit prompts us to aid the world to rebuild, we must, at the same time, construct a better America in which all can share equitably in the blessings of democracy. The Taft–Hartley bill threatens the attainment of this goal. For the sake of this Nation, I hope that this bill will not become law.

Public Papers of the President, Harry S. Truman, 1947, [7], pp. 298–301.

DOCUMENT 11   HARRY S. TRUMAN, ADDRESS BEFORE THE NATIONAL ASSOCIATION FOR THE ADVANCEMENT OF COLORED PEOPLE, 29 JUNE 1947

With this speech, Truman became the first president to address the NAACP, and signaled that he openly would court black Americans in the next election.

It is my deep conviction that we have reached a turning point in the long history of our country's efforts to guarantee freedom and equality to all our citizens. Recent events in the United States and abroad have made us realize that it is more important today than ever before to insure that all Americans enjoy these rights.

When I say all Americans I mean all Americans. ...

We must make the Federal Government a friendly, vigilant defender of the rights of all Americans. And again I mean all Americans. ...

Our immediate task is to remove the last remnants of the barriers which stand between millions of our citizens and their birthright. There is no justifiable reason for discrimination because of ancestry, or religion, or race, or color.

We must not tolerate such limitations on the freedom of any of our people and on their enjoyment of basic rights which every citizen in a truly democratic society must possess.

Every man should have the right to a decent home, the right to an education, the right to adequate medical care, the right to a worthwhile job, the right to an equal share in making public decisions through the ballot box, and the right to a fair trial in a fair court.

We must insure that these rights – on equal terms – are enjoyed by every citizen. To these principles I pledge my full and continued support.

Public Papers of the President, Harry S. Truman, 1947, [7], pp. 311–12.

DOCUMENT 12 ROBERT A. TAFT, US SENATOR FROM OHIO, ADDRESS TO THE WORLD AFFAIRS COUNCIL OF TACOMA, WASHINGTON, 25 SEPTEMBER 1947

One of the leading Republicans attacks the domestic and foreign policies of FDR and Truman as socialistic and naive.

We have won the war, but we have lost the peace. ... President Roosevelt apparently felt that if Mr. Stalin received military aid and kind treatment from England and the United States, he would be transformed into an angel of light, bringing freedom to the world. ... This attitude at Teheran, at Yalta and at Potsdam was promoted apparently by the basic New Deal philosophy which influenced the whole Administration. The general attitude, as exemplified in the influence of the late Mr. Harry Hopkins, was a very friendly one toward communism. Many New Dealers would not go along with Mr. Henry Wallace, who felt that communism was merely another form of democracy; but there were a lot who did have that attitude. ...

As I see it, the Administration was dominated by the 'Mr. Fixit' philosophy of the New Deal. Just as the New Deal wanted to run the lives of all citizens and improve them whether they wished to be improved or not, so they have tried to use our financial resources to force on the rest of the world the manner in which they shall conduct their foreign exchange, their foreign trade, and even their currency and other domestic affairs. No doubt they have acted in good faith in supporting an international control of international trade, but to Europe it looks like an American control trying to boss their affairs. I maintain, therefore, that outside the actual conduct of the war, we could not have made a worse mess of our foreign policy than we did. ...

In communism we face a curious form of aggression. But outside the power of the Russian Army limited to Europe and Asia, it is the battle of ideologies. We cannot fight the ideology of communism with soldiers. ... In general, the battle must be fought out in each country by the people of that country. ... We should meet communism first here in the United States, bring it out into the open and eliminate its influence. If we can't meet it successfully at home, how can we hope to meet it in Europe? Our leaders should speak out in behalf of the American system and get away from the inferiority complex about it we have seen in recent years. The New Dealers really attacked the basic philosophy of American government, its belief in individual and local freedom, in competition and in reward for incentive. They echoed the arguments of Moscow against it, and wanted to move our system well over toward that of Russia. ...

Certainly we wish to help, but an international WPA would fail to solve the problems of world work just as it failed to solve unemployment in the United States. I do not believe America can save the world with money. We can only help the world to save itself if it wishes to be saved and makes its own utmost effort. ... If we can show that this country can maintain freedom and the highest standard of living in the world under the American system, it will not be many years before the example set will be followed by every other nation.

Vital Speeches of the Day, Vol. XIV, 15 October 1947, [14], pp. 16–20.

DOCUMENT 13   CLARK M. CLIFFORD, MEMORANDUM FOR THE PRESIDENT, 19 NOVEMBER 1947

Truman's trusted advisor lays out a blueprint for victory in the 1948 election.

The basic premise of this memorandum – that the Democratic Party is an unhappy alliance of Southern conservatives, Western progressives and Big City labor – is very trite, but very true. And it is equally true that the success or failure of the Democratic leadership can be precisely measured by its ability to lead enough members of these three misfit groups to the polls. ...

It is also very dangerous to assume that the only supporters of Wallace are the Communists. True enough, they give him a disciplined hard-working organization and collect the money to run his campaign. But he also has a large following throughout the country, particularly of the young voters who regard war as the one evil greater than any other. He will also derive support from the pacifists, which means a great number of organized women, and from whatever irreconcilables and die-hard isolationists remain. He will attract votes – and money – from the 'lunatic fringe.' ... Every effort must be made *now* jointly and at one and the same time – although, of course, by different groups – to dissuade him and also to identify him and isolate him in the public mind with the Communists. ...

The farm vote is in most ways identical with the Winning of the West – the Number One Priority. The farmer is at least at present favorably disposed toward the Truman Administration. His crops are good. However the high prices may be affecting the rest of the people, they help him more than hurt him. Parity will protect him – and the Marshall Plan will aid him. ...

President Truman and the Democratic Party cannot win without the *active* support of organized labor. It is dangerous to assume that labor has nowhere else to go in 1948. Labor can stay home. ... The President's veto of the Taft–Hartley Bill, coupled with vehement dislike of the Republicans because they passed it over his veto, does indicate that as of today Labor is friendly to the President. ...

The liberal and progressive leaders are not overly enthusiastic about the Administration. Foreign policy has forced the large bulk to break sharply with Wallace and the fellow-travelers. And, of course, they find no hope in Republican activities as evidenced by the recent Congress. Fear of the Republicans may drive them to activity for President Truman, but at present there is no disposition to do much more than stay home on election day. Whether their reasons are valid or otherwise, many of them feel that the progressive wing has been cut off by the Southerners and the 'organization' leaders from any say in the Democratic Party. This is particularly true of such organizations as Americans for Democratic Action where most of the Roosevelt New Dealers have found haven. ...

Since 1932 when, after intensive work by President Roosevelt, their leaders swung the Pennsylvania Negro block into the Democratic column with the classic remark, 'Turn your picture of Abraham Lincoln to the wall – we have paid that debt,' the northern Negro has voted Democratic (with the exception of 1946 in New York). A theory of many professional politicians is that the northern Negro voter today holds the balance of power in Presidential elections. ... Unless there are real efforts (as distinguished from mere political gestures which are today thoroughly understood and strongly resented by sophisticated Negro leaders), the Negro bloc, which, certainly in Illinois and probably in New York and Ohio, *does* hold the balance of power, will go Republican. ...

Centered in New York City, [the Jewish] vote is normally Democratic and, if large enough, is sufficient to counteract the upstate vote and deliver the state to President Truman. Today the Jewish bloc is interested primarily in Palestine and will continue to be an uncertain quantity right up to the time of the election. ... It will be extremely difficult to decide some of the vexing questions which will arise in the months to come based on political expediency. In the long run, there is likely to be greater gain if the Palestine question is approached on the basis of reaching decisions founded upon intrinsic merit. ...

The Catholic vote is traditionally Democratic. The controlling element in this group today from a political standpoint is the distrust and fear of Communism. ... The attitude of the President and the Administration toward Communism should exert a definite appeal to this group. ...

There is considerable political advantage to the Administration in its battle with the Kremlin. The best guess today is that our poor relations with

Russia will intensify. The nation is already united behind the President on this issue. The worse matters get, up to a fairly certain point – real danger of imminent war – the more is there a sense of crisis. In times of crisis the American citizen tends to back up his President. And on the issue of policy toward Russia, President Truman is comparatively invulnerable to attack because of his brilliant appointment of General Marshall who has convinced the public that as Secretary of State he is nonpartisan and above politics.

In a flank attack tied up with foreign policy, the Republicans have tried to identify the Administration with the domestic Communists. The President adroitly stole their thunder by initiating his own Government employee loyalty investigation procedure and the more frank Republicans admit it. ...

The September 11th speech by Wallace ... appealed to the atavistic fear of 'Wall Street.' This fear is not the sole property of the progressives. It belongs traditionally to the Democratic Party. ... President Truman must carry the West. To carry the West, he must be 'liberal'; he cannot afford to be shackled with the Wall Street label by any so-called progressive movement. ...

The President has a great opportunity of presenting his program to the American people in his message on the State of the Union. He can present his recommendations simply and clearly to the Congress so that the people will know what the President is asking the Congress to do. There is little possibility that he will get much cooperation from the Congress but we want the President to be in a position to receive the credit for whatever they do accomplish while also being in a position to criticize Congress for being obstructionists in failing to comply with other recommendations.

Clark Clifford papers, Harry S. Truman Library, Independence, MO, reprinted in Griffith, [51], pp. 147–53.

DOCUMENT 14   THOMAS E. DEWEY, ADDRESS IN PHILADELPHIA UPON
ACCEPTING THE NOMINATION OF THE REPUBLICAN
NATIONAL CONVENTION, 24 JUNE 1948

The Republican nominee attempts to hold together his party with platitudes and unobjectionable generalities.

Our people are turning away from the meaner things that divide us. They yearn to move to higher ground, to find a common purpose in the finer things which unite us. We must be the instrument of that aspiration. We must be the means by which America's full powers are released and this uncertain future filled again, with opportunity. That is our pledge. That will be the fruit of our victory. ...

We have declared our goal to be a strong and free America in a world of free men – free to speak their own minds, free to develop new ideas, free to publish what they believe, free to move from place to place, free to choose occupations, free to choose and use the fruits of their labor, free to worship God, each according to his own concept of his grace and his mercy. When these rights are secure in the world, the permanent ideals of the Republican party shall have been realized.

The ideals of the American people are the ideals of the Republican party. We have lighted a beacon here in Philadelphia, in this cradle of our own independence. We have lighted a beacon to give eternal hope that men may live in liberty with human dignity and before God and loving Him, stand erect and free.

Vital Speeches of the Day, Vol. XIV, 1 July 1948, [14], pp. 546–8.

DOCUMENT 15   HARRY S. TRUMAN, ADDRESS IN PHILADELPHIA UPON ACCEPTING THE NOMINATION OF THE DEMOCRATIC NATIONAL CONVENTION, 15 JULY 1948

The president unveils the 'give 'em hell' campaign style of his coming campaign.

We have been working together for victory in a great cause. Victory has become a habit of our party. It has been elected four times in succession, and I am convinced it will be elected a fifth time next November. The reason is that the people know that the Democratic Party is the people's party, and the Republican Party is the party of special interest, and it always has been and always will be. ...

I say to labor what I have said to the farmers: they are the most ungrateful people in the world if they pass the Democratic Party by this year.

The total national income has increased from less than $40 billion in 1933 to $203 billion in 1947, the greatest in all the history of the world. These benefits have been spread to all the people, because it is the business of the Democratic Party to see that the people get a fair share of these things. This last, worst 80th Congress proved just the opposite for the Republicans.

The record on foreign policy of the Democratic Party is that the United States has been turned away from isolationism, and we have converted the greatest and best of the Republicans to our viewpoint on that subject. ... We removed trade barriers in the world, which is the best asset we can have for peace. Those trade barriers must not be put back into operation again. ...

As I have said time and time again, foreign policy should be the policy of the whole Nation and not the policy of one party or the other. Partisanship should stop at the water's edge; and I shall continue to preach that through this whole campaign. ...

Now the Republicans came here a few weeks ago, and they wrote a platform. I hope you have all read that platform. They adopted the platform, and that platform had a lot of promises of what the Republican Party is for, and what they would do if they were in power. They promised to do in that platform a lot of the things I have been asking them to do that they have refused to do when they had the power. ...

My duty as president requires that I use every means within my power to get the laws the people need on matters of such importance and urgency. I am therefore calling this Congress back into session July 26th.

On the 26th day of July, which out in Missouri we call 'Turnip Day,' I am going to call Congress back and ask them to pass laws to halt rising prices, to meet the housing crisis – which they are saying they are for in their platform. At the same time I shall ask them to act upon other vitally needed measures such as aid to education, which they say they are for; a national health program, which they say they are for; civil rights legislation, which they say they are for; an increase in the minimum wage, which I doubt very much they are for; extension of the social security coverage and increased benefits, which they say they are for; funds for projects needed in our program to provide public power and cheap electricity. By indirection this 80th Congress has tried to sabotage the power policies the United States has pursued for 14 years. That power lobby is as bad as the real estate lobby, which is sitting on the housing bill.

I shall ask for adequate and decent laws for displaced persons in place of this anti-Semetic, anti-Catholic law which this 80th Congress passed.

Now, my friends, if there is any reality behind that Republican platform, we ought to get some action from a short session of the 80th Congress. They can do this job in 15 days, if they want to do it. They will still have time to go out and run for office. ...

Now, what that worst 80th Congress does in this special session will be the test. The American people will not decide by listening to mere words, or by reading a mere platform. They will decide on the record, the record as it has been written. And in the record is the stark truth, that the battle lines of 1948 are the same as they were in 1932, when the Nation lay prostrate and helpless as a result of Republican misrule and inaction.

In 1932 we were attacking the citadel of special privilege and greed. We were fighting to drive the money changers out of the temple. Today, in 1948, we are now the defenders of the stronghold of democracy and equal opportunity, the haven of the ordinary people of this land and not of the favored classes or the powerful few. The battle cry is the same now as it was in 1932. ...

Public Papers of the President, Harry S. Truman, 1948, [7], pp. 406–10.

*The triumphant Truman asks Congress to implement his liberal 'Fair Deal'
agenda.*

In this society, we are conservative about the values and principles which we
cherish; but we are forward-looking in protecting those values and principles
and extending their benefits. We have rejected the discredited theory that the
fortunes of the Nation should be in the hands of a privileged few. We have
abandoned the 'trickle-down' concept of national prosperity. Instead, we
believe that our economic system should rest on a democratic foundation
and that wealth should be created for the benefit of all.

The recent election shows that the people of the United States are in
favor of this kind of society and want to go on improving it.

The American people have decided that poverty is just as wasteful and
just as unnecessary as preventable disease. We have pledged our common
resources to help one another in the hazards and struggles of individual life.
We believe that no unfair prejudice or artificial distinction should bar any
citizen of the United States of America from an education, or from good
health, or from a job that he is capable of performing. ...

Our first great opportunity is to protect our economy against the evils of
'boom and bust.'

This objective cannot be attained by government alone. Indeed, the
greater part of the task must be performed by individual efforts under our
system of free enterprise. We can keep our present prosperity, and increase
it, only if free enterprise and free government work together to that end. We
cannot afford to float along ceaselessly on a postwar boom until it collapses.
It is not enough merely to prepare to weather a recession if it comes. Instead,
government and business must work together constantly to achieve more
and more jobs and more and more production – which mean more and more
prosperity for all the people. ...

At present, the working men and women of the Nation are unfairly dis-
criminated against by a statute that abridges their rights, curtails their con-
structive efforts, and hampers our system of free collective bargaining. That
statute is the Labor–Management Relations Act of 1947, sometimes called
the Taft–Hartley Act.

That act should be repealed! ...

The health of our economy and its maintenance at high levels further
require that the minimum wage fixed by law should be raised to at least 75
cents an hour. ...

Standards of living on the farm should be just as good as anywhere else in the country. Farm price supports are an essential part of our program to achieve these ends. ...

The present coverage of the social security laws is altogether inadequate; the benefit payments are too low. One-third of our workers are not covered. ... We should expand our social security program, both as to the size of the benefits and the extent of coverage, against the economic hazards due to unemployment, old age, sickness, and disability.

We must spare no effort to raise the general level of health in this country. In a nation as rich as ours, it is a shocking fact that tens of millions lack adequate medical care. We are short of doctors, hospitals, nurses. We must remedy these shortages. Moreover, we need – and we must have without further delay – a system of prepaid medical insurance which will enable every American to afford good medical care.

It is equally shocking that millions of our children are not receiving a good education. Millions of them are in overcrowded, obsolete buildings. We are short of teachers ... I cannot repeat too strongly my desire for prompt Federal financial aid to the States to help them operate and maintain their school systems. ...

The civil rights proposals I made to the 80th Congress, I now repeat to the 81st Congress. They should be enacted in order that the Federal Government may assume the leadership and discharge the obligations clearly placed upon it by the Constitution. I stand squarely behind those proposals. ...

I hope for cooperation from farmers, from labor, and from business. Every segment of our population and every individual has a right to expect from our Government a fair deal.

Public Papers of the President, Harry S. Truman, 1949, [7], pp. 1–7.

DOCUMENT 17   EXCERPTS OF THE PROCEEDINGS OF THE US SENATE, 25 JANUARY 1950

Several Senators criticize the Truman administration regarding Alger Hiss, Dean Acheson, and China policy, demonstrating the collapse of bipartisan foreign policy and the intersection of the internal security issue and foreign policy.

Senator Joseph McCarthy: I wonder if the Senator is aware of a most fantastic statement the Secretary of State made in the last few minutes. At a press conference he was asked to comment on the conviction of Alger Hiss. ... This is what Dean Acheson said: 'Regardless of the outcome of the appeal, I shall never turn my back on Alger Hiss.'

Senator Karl Mundt: ... I am not greatly concerned about what influence Alger Hiss has on the position of Dean Acheson's back but a great many Americans are concerned about the degree of influence Hiss may have had upon the position of Dean Acheson's mind. ...

Senator Homer Capehart: I am now more proud then ever of the fact that I voted against his confirmation. ...

Senator Joseph McCarthy: Would the Senator think the statement I have read might be an indication that the Secretary of State is also telling the world that he will not turn his back on any other of the Communists in the State Department?. ...

Senator Karl Mundt: ... one rightfully wonders concerning the influence of Alger Hiss in the State Department in the formation of our policy toward China which has resulted in the disastrous collapse of autonomous China and the complete domination of that once great ally of ours by the Moscow-supported armies of communism.

Congressional Record, Vol. 96, Part 1, 81st Congress, [11], pp. 895–903.

DOCUMENT 18   NATIONAL SECURITY COUNCIL PAPER NO. 68 (NSC-68), 7 APRIL 1950

American cold war policy shifts to a more military posture in the aftermath of the Soviet atomic bomb test and the triumph of the Chinese Communists.

The issues that face us are momentous, involving the fulfillment or destruction not only of this Republic but of civilization itself. They are issues which will not await our deliberations. With conscience and resolution this Government and the people must now take new and fateful decisions. ...

The assault on free institutions is world-wide now, and in the context of the present polarization of power a defeat of free institutions anywhere is a defeat everywhere. ... Thus unwillingly our free society finds itself mortally challenged by the Soviet system. ...

Our overall policy at the present time may be described as one designed to foster a world environment in which the American system can survive and flourish. ... This broad intention embraces two subsidiary policies. One is a policy which we would probably pursue even if there were no Soviet threat. It is a policy of attempting to develop a healthy international community. The other is the policy of 'containing' the Soviet Union. These two policies are closely interrelated and interact with one another. Nevertheless, the distinction between them is basically valid and contributes to a clearer understanding of what we are trying to do. ...

It was and continues to be cardinal in this [containment] policy that we possess superior overall power in ourselves or in dependable combination with other like-minded nations. One of the most important ingredients of power is military strength. ... In the face of obviously mounting Soviet military strength ours has declined relatively. Partly as a byproduct of this, but also for other reasons, we now find ourselves at a diplomatic impasse with the Soviet Union, with the Kremlin growing bolder, with both of us holding on grimly to what we have and with ourselves facing difficult decisions.

It is apparent from the preceding sections that the integrity and vitality of our system is in greater jeopardy than ever before in our history. ... It is quite clear from Soviet theory and practice that the Kremlin seeks to bring the free world under its dominion by the methods of the cold war. The preferred technique is to subvert by infiltration and intimidation. ... At the same time the Soviet Union is seeking to create overwhelming military force, in order to back up infiltration with intimidation. In the only terms in which it understands strength, it is seeking to demonstrate to the free world that force and the will to use it are on the side of the Kremlin, that those who lack it are decadent and doomed. In local incidents it threatens and encroaches both for the sake of political gains and to increase the anxiety and defeatism in the free world. ...

A more rapid build-up of political, economic and military strength and thereby confidence in the free world than is now contemplated is the only course which is consistent with progress toward achieving our fundamental purpose. The frustration of the Kremlin design requires the free world to develop a successfully functioning political and economic system and a vigorous political offensive against the Soviet Union. These, in turn, require an adequate military shield under which they can develop. It is necessary to have the military power to deter, if possible, Soviet expansionism, and to defeat, if necessary, aggressive Soviet or Soviet-directed actions of a limited or total character. ...

It is imperative that this trend be reversed by a much more rapid and concerted build-up of the actual strength of both the United States and the other nations of the free world. The analysis shows that this will be costly and will involve significant domestic financial and economic adjustments. ...

A comprehensive and decisive program to win the peace and frustrate the Kremlin design should be so designed that it can be sustained for as long as necessary to achieve our national objectives. It would probably involve:

1. The development of an adequate political and economic framework for the achievement of our long-range objectives.
2. A substantial increase in expenditures for military purposes. ...

3. A substantial increase in military assistance programs, designed to foster cooperative efforts, which will adequately and efficiently meet the requirements of our allies. ...

4. Some increase in economic assistance programs and recognition of the need to continue these programs until their purposes have been accomplished.

5. A concerted attack on the problem of the United States balance of payments, along the lines already approved by the President.

6. Development of programs designed to build and maintain confidence among other peoples in our strength and resolution, and to wage overt psychological warfare calculated to encourage mass defections from Soviet allegiance and to frustrate the Kremlin design in other ways.

7. Intensification of affirmative and timely measures and operations by covert means in the fields of economic warfare and political and psychological warfare with a view to fomenting and supporting unrest and revolt in selected strategic satellite countries.

8. Development of internal security and civilian defense programs.

9. Improvement and intensification of intelligence activities.

10. Reduction of Federal expenditures for purposes other than defense and foreign assistance, if necessary by the deferment of certain desirable programs.

11. Increased taxes. ...

The whole success of the proposed program hangs ultimately on recognition by this Government, the American people, and all free peoples, that the cold war is in fact a real war in which the survival of the free world is at stake.

US Department of State, *Foreign Relations of the United States, 1950, Vol. I, National Security Affairs; Foreign Economic Policy*, [12], pp. 234–315.

DOCUMENT 19   **HARRY S. TRUMAN, STATEMENT ON RELIEVING GENERAL DOUGLAS MACARTHUR OF HIS COMMAND, 11 APRIL 1951**

The president fires MacArthur, producing a fire storm of protest and calls for the president's resignation.

With deep regret I have concluded that General of the Army Douglas MacArthur is unable to give his wholehearted support to the policies of the United States Government and of the United Nations in matters pertaining to his official duties. In view of the specific responsibilities imposed upon me by the Constitution of the United States and the added responsibility which has been entrusted to me by the United Nations, I have decided that I must make a change of command in the Far East. I have, therefore, relieved General MacArthur of his commands and have designated Lt. Gen. Mathew B. Ridgway as his successor.

Full and vigorous debate on matters of national policy is a vital element in the constitutional system of our free democracy. It is fundamental, however, that military commanders must be governed by the policies and directives issued to them in the manner provided by our laws and Constitution. In time of crisis, this consideration is particularly compelling.

Public Papers of the President, Harry S. Truman, 1951, [7], p. 22.

DOCUMENT 20	DOUGLAS MACARTHUR'S ADDRESS TO A JOINT SESSION OF THE US CONGRESS, 19 APRIL 1951

The retiring general criticizes administration policy in Korea.

I know war as few other men now living know it, and nothing to me is more revolting. I have long advocated its complete abolition, as its very destructiveness on both friend and foe has rendered it useless as a means of settling international disputes. ... But once war is forced upon us, there is no other alternative than to apply every available means to bring it to a swift end. War's very object is victory not prolonged indecision. In war there is no substitute for victory. ...

There are some who for varying reasons would appease Red China. ... Some may say to avoid spread of the conflict into an all-out war with China. Others, to avoid Soviet intervention. Neither explanation seems valid, for China is already engaging with the maximum power it can commit, and the Soviet will not necessarily mesh its actions with our moves. Like a cobra, any new enemy will more likely strike whenever it feels that the relativity in military or other potential is in its favor on a world-wide basis.

The tragedy of Korea is further heightened by the fact that as military action is confined to its territorial limits, it condemns that nation, which it is our purpose to save, to suffer the devastating impact of full naval and air bombardment while the enemy's sanctuaries are fully protected from such attack and devastation. Of the nations of the world, Korea alone, up to now, is the sole one which has risked its all against communism. The magnificence of the courage and fortitude of the Korean people defies description. They have chosen to risk death rather than slavery. Their last words to me were 'Don't scuttle the Pacific.' ...

I am closing my fifty-two years of military service. When I joined the Army, even before the turn of the century, it was the fulfillment of all my boyish hopes and dreams. The world has turned over many times since I took the oath on the plain at West Point, and the hopes and dreams have long since vanished, but I still remember the refrain of one of the most popular barrack ballads of that day, which proclaimed most proudly, that 'old soldiers never die, they just fade away.'

And like the old soldier of that ballad, I now close my military career and just fade away, an old soldier who tried to do his duty as God gave him the light to see that duty. Goodbye.

Vital Speeches of the Day, Vol. XVII, 1 May 1951, [14], pp. 432–3.

DOCUMENT 21   DWIGHT D. EISENHOWER, REPUBLICAN NOMINEE FOR PRESIDENT, ADDRESS TO THE PEOPLE OF BOISE, IDAHO, 20 AUGUST 1952

Eisenhower argues for a 'middle way' in American politics, reflecting acceptance of the New Deal but opposition to its expansion.

Now, ladies and gentlemen, this middle way today starts off with certain very definite assumptions. It assumes that all Americans of all parties have now accepted and will forever support what we call social gains, the security that people are entitled to in their old age and to make certain they are adequately cared for, insurance against unemployment, equal opportunities for everybody regardless of race, religion, where he was born or what is his national origin.

We have accepted a moral obligation – the education of our young, decent housing, the rights of working men and working women to be productive, the rights of each of us to earn what he can and to save it as far as taxes will let him. We accept that as part of these social gains the fact that Americans must have adequate insurance against disaster.

No one counts that thing a political issue any more. That is part of America. ... Let's call all those things just a solid floor that keeps all of us from falling into the pit of disaster. But on top of that floor, let's not interfere with the incentive, the ambition, the right of any of you to build the most glorious structure on top of that floor that you can imagine. ...

Now, we have had for a long time a Government that applies the philosophy of the left to the Government. The Government will build the power dams, the Government will tell you how to distribute your power, the Government will do this and that. The Government does everything, but come and wash the dishes for the housewife. Now their answer to evils in Government is more Government. ...

I should like to pledge to you that all my efforts will be devoted to see that we can have a Government that does not grow complacent, that does not grow away from the people and become indifferent to them, that does not become arrogant in the exercise of its powers, but strives to be the partner and servant of the people and not their master. One that does not grow indifferent to your problems, to the problems of any American, that does not create resentment.

Now, ladies and gentlemen, these things must develop when any one party is too long in power. It is so sure of its position that it does not have to uproot the first sign of dishonesty in Government. It goes along and thinks, never mind, that will be alright. ... The American people have a right to demand the best.

Vital Speeches of the Day, Vol. XVIII, 9 September 1952, [14], pp. 677–8.

CHRONOLOGY

1945

12 April	Death of Franklin D. Roosevelt; Harry S. Truman becomes President of the United States.
23 April	Truman's meeting with Soviet Foreign Minister Molotov.
8 May	Germany surrenders unconditionally; V-E (Victory in Europe) Day.
17 July–2 Aug.	Potsdam Conference of the Big Three: the United States, Great Britain and the Soviet Union.
6 Aug.	The United States drops an atomic bomb on Hiroshima, Japan.
8 Aug.	The Soviet Union declares war on Japan.
9 Aug.	The United States drops an atomic bomb on Nagasaki, Japan.
15 Aug.	Japan surrenders unconditionally; V-J (Victory in Japan) Day.
6 Sept.	Truman presents the 21-point plan for Reconversion to Congress.
11 Sept.–2 Oct.	London Conference of the Big Three foreign ministers.
16–26 Dec.	Moscow Conference of the Big Three foreign ministers.

1946

20 Feb.	Truman signs Full Employment Act.
22 Feb.	George Kennan sends his 'Long Telegram.'
5 March	Winston Churchill's 'Iron Curtain' speech at Fulton, Missouri.
23 July	Henry Wallace criticizes US foreign policy in a letter to Truman.
19 Sept.	Truman asks for and receives Wallace's resignation.
5 Nov.	Republicans win control of Congress.
25 Nov.	Truman establishes the Temporary Commission on Employee Loyalty.

1947

24 Feb.	Britain informs the United States that it can no longer support the Greek government.
12 March	Truman delivers his 'Truman Doctrine' speech to Congress.
21 March	Truman issues Executive Order 9835 creating the Federal Employee Loyalty Program.

22 May	Truman signs the 'Truman Doctrine' appropriation by Congress for Greece and Turkey.
5 June	George Marshall invites European nations to participate in the 'Marshall Plan.'
16 June	Truman vetoes income tax cut.
20 June	Truman vetoes Taft–Hartley Act.
23 June	Congress overrides Truman's veto of the Taft–Hartley Act.
29 June	Truman becomes the first president to address the NAACP.
26 July	Congress passes the National Security Act.
20–30 Oct.	HUAC hearings on the movie industry.

1948

24 Feb.	*Coup d'état* brings communists to power in Czechoslovakia.
2 April	Congress approves the European Recovery Program (the Marshall Plan).
14 May	Truman recognizes the state of Israel.
24 June	The Soviet Union imposes a full blockade on West Berlin.
28 June	Thomas E. Dewey accepts the Republican Party nomination for president.
15 July	Truman accepts the Democratic Party nomination for president.
20 July	US Communist Party leaders are indicted for violating the Smith Act of 1940.
26 July	Truman calls a special session of the 80th Congress.
30 July	Truman issues an executive order desegregating the Armed Forces.
2 Nov.	Truman is elected president in his own right.

1949

5 Jan.	Truman presents his Fair Deal proposals to Congress in the State of the Union address.
4 April	Twelve nations in Europe and North America sign the North Atlantic Treaty.
5 May	Soviet Union announces it will lift the Berlin blockade.
21 July	The US Senate ratifies NATO.
6 Aug.	The State Department issues its 'White Paper' on China.
24 Sept.	Truman announces that the Soviet Union has detonated an atomic device.
1 Oct.	In Beijing, Mao Zedong proclaims the establishment of the People's Republic of China.

14 Oct.	Eleven top US Communist Party officials are convicted of violating the Smith Act and sentenced to prison.
26 Oct.	Congress approves a minimum wage increase from 40 cents to 75 cents an hour, effective from January 1950.

1950

22 Jan.	Alger Hiss is convicted of perjury.
31 Jan.	Truman announces that the United States will develop a hydrogen bomb.
4 Feb.	Klaus Fuchs is arrested, accused of passing atomic secrets to the Soviet Union.
9 Feb.	Senator Joseph McCarthy makes a speech in Wheeling, West Virginia, charging that there are 205 known communists in the State Department.
14 Feb.	Sino-Soviet alliance is signed by Mao and Stalin.
7 April	The National Security Council sends NSC-68 to the president.
25 June	The North Korean Army invades South Korea.
27 June	United Nations resolutions are passed, calling for assistance to South Korea to repel the North Korean invasion.
28 Aug.	The Social Security Act is amended to expand coverage and increase benefits.
15 Sept.	The Inchon operation begins the reversal of American retreat in Korea.
22 Sept.	Truman vetoes the Internal Security (McCarran) Act.
23 Sept.	Internal Security (McCarran) Act passes over Truman's veto.
1 Nov.	An assassination attempt against Truman fails.
7 Nov.	Republicans make significant gains in the Congressional elections.
26 Nov.	A massive Chinese counteroffensive against the American advance in North Korea begins.
15 Dec.	Truman declares a state of national emergency and imposes wage and price controls.

1951

26 Feb.	The Twenty-second Amendment to the Constitution is ratified, limiting future presidents to two terms.
21 March	Julius and Ethel Rosenberg are convicted of atomic espionage.
11 April	Truman relieves General Douglas MacArthur of command in Korea.
19 April	MacArthur addresses a joint session of Congress.

1952

29 March	Truman announces that he will not be a candidate for re-election.
11 July	Dwight Eisenhower receives the Republican nomination for president.
26 July	Adlai Stevenson receives the Democratic nomination for president.
1 Nov.	The United States explodes the first hydrogen bomb.
4 Nov.	Eisenhower is elected president.

1953

20 Jan.	Harry Truman leaves the White House and returns to his home in Independence, MO.

GLOSSARY

Amerasia case (June 1945) Espionage case in which a left-wing magazine was found to possess classified government documents; an early cause of the Red Scare.

Americans for Democratic Action (ADA) Mainstream group within the Democratic Party, which, while critical of Truman's domestic leadership, supported his anti-communist foreign policy.

Appeasement Policy pursued in the 1930s by Britain and France to try to avoid war with Nazi Germany. Blamed for encouraging Hitler's aggression, it became synonymous with weak and counterproductive diplomacy which made war more rather than less likely.

'*Asia First*' Foreign policy position, most often held by Republicans and former isolationists, that American diplomacy should focus on Asia rather than Europe.

'*Baby boom*' The dramatic up-turn in births after World War II, which created a distinctive postwar generation.

Berlin blockade Attempt by the Soviet Union, beginning in June 1948, to force the Western powers out of West Berlin. Successfully countered by the Berlin airlift, and ended in May 1949.

Bolshevik Revolution (1917) Led by Lenin, it brought the Communist Party to power in Russia, which became known as the Soviet Union.

Central Intelligence Agency (CIA) Created by the National Security Act in 1947, the first peacetime intelligence agency in American history. Charged with co-ordinating and analysing all intelligence, as well as conducting covert operations.

Cold war liberalism A more conservative position than New Deal liberalism, it accepted the fundamental soundness of the American political and economic system (thus seeing no need for basic reform), and saw the greatest challenges to the United States not at home but abroad.

Congress of Industrial Organizations (CIO) Liberal, national union organization which purged its communist members during the early cold war.

Containment First articulated by George Kennan, the policy of using American economic, political and eventually military power to prevent the spread of Soviet power and influence.

Dixiecrat Party Splinter group, led by South Carolina Governor Strom Thurmond, which broke with the Democratic Party in 1948 over the issue of civil rights, a sign of the future problems for the Democrats in the south.

Equal Rights Amendment (ERA) Proposed amendment to the Constitution which would have prohibited any discrimination based on sex. Failed to pass Congress in the Truman years.

Executive Order 9835   Created the Federal Employee Loyalty Program on 21 March 1947.

Fair Employment Practices Commission (FEPC)   Established on a temporary basis by FDR during World War II to prevent racial discrimination in war industries, Truman's proposal for a permanent body was not approved by Congress.

Federal Employee Loyalty Program   Instituted by Truman in March 1947 in response to charges that communists had infiltrated the US government, it put the burden on the accused to prove his/her loyalty.

'Fellow travelers'   Label given to people who did not join the Communist Party but sympathized with its goals.

'Fifth columnists'   Term used to describe communist agents within the United States who would serve the Soviet Union in case of war.

Full Employment Act (1946)   Legislation which called for 'maximum' rather than 'full' employment, making it clear that despite its original intention, employment would not be the sole concern of economic policy. Nonetheless, it was also an official acceptance of the concept that government had an obligation to manage the economy.

GI Bill   Passed toward the end of World War II, it subsidized the housing, education, training, and businesses of millions of returning veterans and helped ease the reconversion to a peacetime economy.

House Committee on Un-American Activities (HUAC)   Established in the late 1930s to investigate Nazis in the United States, it shifted its focus to communists and became an important actor in the Red Scare.

'Iron Curtain' speech (March 1946)   Given by former Prime Minister Winston Churchill in Fulton, Missouri, it called for an Anglo-American alliance against the Soviet Union.

Isolationism   American tradition of avoiding political and military involvement in European affairs, seriously diminished by World War II and the cold war.

Jim Crow segregation   The practice of legal separation of the races in Southern states, the focus of the civil rights movement in the 1940s and 1950s.

Levittown   A suburban community that was quickly built after World War II, which made home ownership widely available to the middle class. The result of mass production techniques applied to the housing industry, it was a major factor in the growth of suburbs.

Liberal consensus   Term used to describe the convergence of the policies of the two major political parties by the early 1950s. Its major components were an acceptance of an internationalist foreign policy and of the limited welfare state created by the New Deal in the 1930s.

Limited welfare state   The basic economic protections created by the Social Security system: old age pensions, unemployment insurance, disability insurance, etc.

Long Telegram   Written in 1946 by State Department official George Kennan in Moscow, it set the foundation for the policy of containment.

Manhattan Project   The secret effort in World War II to produce an atomic bomb.

Marshall Plan   A massive economic assistance program for Western Europe, also known as the European Recovery Program (ERP). Succeeded in both reviving the economies of the region and blunting the appeal of communism.

McCarthyism   Named after Senator Joseph McCarthy, came to mean the tactic of attacking political enemies by charging them (often without any evidence) with being either communists or sympathetic to communism.

Modern Republicanism   Eisenhower's position in 1952, combining traditional Republican conservatism and fiscal discipline with an acceptance of the permanency of Social Security and other New Deal reforms.

Monroe Doctrine   An American foreign policy tradition, first enunciated by President James Monroe in 1823, that the western hemisphere is off limits to European interference.

National Association for the Advancement of Colored People (NAACP)   Founded in 1909, an influential civil rights group which flourished in the 1940s and 1950s, and led the judicial effort to outlaw segregation.

National Security Act of 1947 (NSA)   A major reorganization of the American foreign policy institutions of the executive branch, it placed the military under a single Secretary of Defense, and created the National Security Council and the Central Intelligence Agency.

National Security Council (NSC)   Created by the National Security Act of 1947, it consisted of the president, vice-president, secretaries of state and defense and others to co-ordinate national security policy.

National Security Council Paper No. 68 (NSC-68)   Influential policy paper which called for the militarization of the cold war through increased defense spending.

'National security state'   Label given to the growing governmental apparatus of defense and intelligence, growing out of the heightened American concern with threats from without and within during the cold war.

New Deal liberalism   Prominent in the 1930s and on the wane in the 1940s and 1950s, it saw the need for widespread reform and change, with a large role for government to play in regulating the American economy.

Open Door policy   American foreign policy tradition of seeking to expand its trade with other nations, formally declared by the US government regarding China in 1900.

Potsdam Conference (July–August 1945)   Meeting of wartime allies Truman, Stalin and Churchill (later replaced by Attlee), to settle the fate of postwar Europe.

Reconstruction   The period following the American Civil War, from 1865 to 1877, during which the states which had seceded from the Union were gradually brought back to full and equal stature in the American Union, and regained the right of self-rule, usually after a period of military occupation.

Red scare   The fear of communist espionage and infiltration which gripped the United States in the late 1940s and early 1950s.

Shelly vs Kramer (1948)   Supreme Court ruling that state courts could not enforce restrictive clauses in private contracts. Still, the practice continued informally, making real integration of northern neighborhoods slow.

Taft–Hartley Act (1947)   Anti-union legislation which gave the president authority to order an 80-day cooling-off period when the national interest demanded. It outlawed the closed shop, allowed state right-to-work laws and federal injunctions against strikes, and required union leaders to swear that they were not communists.

Tennessee Valley Authority (TVA)   A New Deal project which brought electricity to a large region surrounding the Tennessee Valley. Often cited by liberals as an example of the power of the federal government to do things which improve the lives of people, and which private industry cannot do.

Totalitarianism   System of government in which the state has complete control over the lives of its citizenry, such as Hitler's Germany or Stalin's Soviet Union.

Truman Doctrine (1947)   The president's declaration to Congress that it must be the policy of the United States to resist aggression or internal subversion against free nations. It was the first clear, public statement of containment.

'White Paper' (1949)   An explanation of recent American relations with China, in which the State Department argued that there was nothing the United States could have done which would have prevented the victory of the Communists in the Chinese civil war.

Yalta Conference (February 1945)   Meeting of FDR, Stalin and Churchill to discuss postwar plans for Europe. It later became the focus of charges that FDR had 'sold out' eastern Europe to the Soviets because of compromises made there which made Soviet domination of the area all but certain.

WHO'S WHO

Acheson, Dean Secretary of State, 1949–53. Also served as assistant secretary of state, 1945–47. One of Truman's trusted advisors.

Byrnes, James F. Democratic politician from South Carolina, considered by FDR for the vice-presidential nomination in 1944; Secretary of State, 1945–47.

Chiang Kai-shek Nationalist leader of China in the 1930s and 1940s. After losing the Chinese civil war to the Communists in 1949, he and his government fled to Taiwan and established themselves there, claiming to be still the legitimate government of China.

Churchill, Winston Prime minister of Great Britain during World War II. Lost power in elections held in August 1945. Remained an influential statesman; returned to power in 1951.

Clifford, Clark Naval aide to President Truman, became an influential advisor on both domestic and foreign policy.

Dewey, Thomas Governor of New York, Republican nominee for president, 1944 and 1948.

Eisenhower, Dwight D. Commander of the D-Day (6 June 1944) invasion of Normandy; Supreme Commander of NATO, 1950–52; successful Republican candidate for president in 1952.

Hiss, Alger State Department official named by Whittaker Chambers as a Soviet agent, convicted of perjury in January 1950 for denying passing documents to Chambers.

Hoover, Herbert President of the United States, 1929–33; influential Republican leader.

Hoover, J. Edgar Director of the FBI; aggressive anti-communist.

Ickes, Harold Interior Secretary, 1933–46; a leading voice of New Deal liberalism.

Kennan, George F. Soviet expert in the State Department; served in US Embassy in Moscow and as the head of the Policy Planning Staff; author of the 'Long Telegram' and the containment policy.

Kim Il Sung Pro-Soviet, communist leader of North Korea.

MacArthur, Douglas Commander of American forces in Asia during World War II, head of the occupation forces in Japan after the war, and commander of UN forces during the Korean War, June 1950–April 1951. Fired by President Truman for insubordination.

Mao Zedong Chairman of the Chinese Communist Party; leader of China after 1949.

Marshall, George C. Army Chief of Staff in World War II; Secretary of State, 1947–49; Secretary of Defense, 1950–52.

McCarthy, Joseph   Republican Senator from Wisconsin, 1946–56, became well known for his charges of communists in the US government.

Molotov, Vyacheslav   Foreign minister of the Soviet Union during World War II and the early cold war years.

Nixon, Richard M.   Republican member of the House from California, 1946–50; Senator from California, 1950–52; successful vice-presidential nominee in 1952. Came to public prominence as a member of HUAC who pursued the Alger Hiss case.

Roosevelt, Franklin D.   President of the United States, 1933–45.

Rosenberg, Julius   Along with his wife, Ethel, charged and convicted of passing atomic secrets to the Soviet Union. The couple was executed by electric chair in 1953.

Stalin, Joseph   Leader of the Soviet Union throughout World War II and the Truman years.

Stevenson, Adlai   Governor of Illinois; unsuccessful Democratic nominee for president in 1952.

Syngman Rhee   Pro-western, anti-communist leader of South Korea.

Taft, Robert   Senator from Ohio, son of former President William Howard Taft; leader of the conservative, isolationist wing of the Republican Party. Sought the 1952 Republican nomination, but lost it to Eisenhower.

Thurmond, Strom   Governor of South Carolina, split with the Democratic Party in 1948 over its civil rights advocacy and ran for president on the Dixiecrat Party ticket.

Truman, Harry S.   President of the United States, 1945–53.

Vandenberg, Arthur   Republican Senator who converted to internationalism; chairman of the Senate Foreign Relations Committee, 1947–49

Wallace, Henry A.   Vice-president of the United States, 1941–45; Secretary of Commerce, 1945–46. Leader of the left-wing of the Democratic Party, split with the party in 1948 and ran for president on the Progressive Party ticket.

BIBLIOGRAPHY

PRIMARY SOURCES

1 Acheson, Dean, *Present at the Creation: My Years in the State Department*, W. W. Norton & Co., New York, 1969.

2 Bohlen, Charles, *Witness to History 1929–1969*, W.W. Norton & Co., New York, 1973.

3 Churchill, Winston, *Triumph and Tragedy*, Houghton Mifflin, Boston, MA, 1954.

4 Clifford, Clark, with Richard Holbrooke, *Counsel to the President: A Memoir*, Random House, New York, 1991.

5 Ferrell, Robert H. (ed.), *Off the Record: The Private Papers of Harry S. Truman*, Penguin, New York, 1980.

6 Judge, Edward H. and John W. Langdon (eds), *The Cold War: A History through Documents*, Prentice-Hall, Upper Saddle River, NJ, 1999.

7 *Public Papers of the Presidents of the United States, Harry S. Truman*, 8 vols, 1945–1952, Office of the Federal Register, National Archives and Record Service, Washington, DC, 1961–66.

8 Schlesinger, Arthur M., *The Vital Center: The Politics of Freedom*, Houghton Mifflin Co., Boston, MA, 1949.

9 Truman, Harry S., *Memoirs, Vol. 1, Years of Decisions*, Doubleday, Garden City, NY, 1955.

10 Truman, Harry S., *Memoirs, Vol. 2., Years of Trial and Hope*, Doubleday, Garden City, NY, 1956.

11 US Congress, *Congressional Record*, US Government Printing Office, Washington, DC, 1950.

12 US Department of State, *Foreign Relations of the United States*, various years and volumes, US Government Printing Office, Washington, DC, 1969–77.

13 US House of Representatives, Committee on Un-American Activities, *Hearings, Regarding the Communist Infiltration of the Motion Picture Industry, October 20–30, 1947*, US Government Printing Office, Washington, DC, 1947.

14 *Vital Speeches of the Day*, The City News Publishing Co., New York, vols xiv–xviii, 1947–52.

SECONDARY SOURCES

15 Abel, Jules, *The Truman Scandals*, Regnery, Chicago, IL, 1956.

16 Allen, Thomas B. and Norman Polmar, *Code-Name Downfall: The Secret Plan to Invade Japan*, Simon & Schuster, New York, 1996.

17 Alperovitz, Gar, *Atomic Diplomacy: Hiroshima and Potsdam and the American Confrontation with Soviet Power*, Vintage Books, New York, 1967.

18   Alperovitz, Gar, *The Decision to Use the Atomic Bomb and the Architecture of an American Myth*, Alfred A. Knopf, New York, 1995.
19   Ambrose, Stephen, E., *Rise to Globalism: American Foreign Policy since 1938*, 6th edn, Penguin, New York, 1991.
20   Berman, William C., *The Politics of Civil Rights in the Truman Administration*, Ohio State University Press, Columbus, OH, 1970.
21   Bernstein, Barton J. (ed.), *Politics and Policies of the Truman Administration*, Quadrangle Books, Chicago, IL, 1970.
22   Bernstein, Barton J. and Allen J. Matusow (eds), *The Truman Administration: A Documentary History*, Harper and Row, New York, 1966.
23   Black, Allida M., *Casting Her Own Shadow: Eleanor Roosevelt and the Shaping of Postwar Liberalism*, Columbia University Press, New York, 1996.
24   Blair, Clay, *The Forgotten War, America in Korea 1950–1953*, Times Books, New York, 1987.
25   Blum, John M., *V was for Victory: Politics and American Culture during World War II*, Harcourt Brace Jovanovich, New York, 1976.
26   Blum, Robert M., *Drawing the Line: The Origins of American Containment Policy in East Asia*, W. W. Norton & Co., New York, 1982.
27   Boyer, Paul, *By the Bomb's Early Light*, Pantheon, New York, 1985.
28   Brinkley, Alan, *The End of Reform: New Deal Liberalism in Recession and War*, Alfred A. Knopf, New York, 1995.
29   Caute, David, *The Great Fear: The Anti-Communist Purge under Truman and Eisenhower*, Simon & Schuster, New York, 1978.
30   Chafe, William H., *The Unfinished Journey: America since World War II*, 4th edn, Oxford University Press, New York, 1999.
31   Chafe, William H. and Harvard Sitkoff (eds), *A History of Our Time: Readings on Postwar America*, 4th edn, Oxford University Press, New York, 1995.
32   Cochran, Bert, *Harry Truman and the Crisis Presidency*, Funk and Wagnalls, New York, 1973.
33   Cohen, Warren, *America's Response to China: A History of Sino-American Relations*, 3rd edn, Columbia University Press, New York, 1990.
34   Cumings, Bruce, *The Origins of the Korean War*, 2 vols, Princeton University Press, Princeton, NJ, 1981–90.
35   Divine, Robert A., *Foreign Policy and Presidential Elections: Vol. 1, 1940–1948*, New Viewpoints, New York, 1974.
36   Donovan, Robert, J., *Conflict and Crisis: The Presidency of Harry Truman, 1945–1948*, W. W. Norton, & Co., New York, 1977.
37   Donovan, Robert, J., *Tumultuous Years: The Presidency of Harry Truman, 1949–1953*, W. W. Norton & Co., New York, 1982.
38   Donovan, Robert J., *Nemesis: Truman and Johnson in the Coils of War in Asia*, St Martin's-Marek, New York, 1984.
39   Druks, Herbert, *Harry S. Truman and the Russians, 1945–1953*, R. Speller, New York, 1966.
40   Dunar, Andrew J., *The Truman Scandals and the Politics of Morality*, University of Missouri Press, Columbia, MO, 1984.
41   Feis, Herbert, *Between War and Peace: The Potsdam Conference*, Princeton University Press, Princeton, NJ, 1960.

42 Feis, Herbert, *The Atomic Bomb and the End of World War II*, Princeton University Press, Princeton, NJ, 1970.

43 Ferrell, Robert H., *Harry S. Truman and the Modern American Presidency*, Little Brown, Boston, MA, 1983.

44 Ferrell, Robert H., *Harry S. Truman: A Life*, University of Missouri Press, Columbia, MO, 1994.

45 Freeland, Richard M., *The Truman Doctrine and the Origins of McCarthyism: Foreign Policy, Domestic Politics and Internal Security, 1946–1948*, Alfred A. Knopf, New York, 1972.

46 Fried, Richard M., *Nightmare in Red: The McCarthy Era in Perspective*, Oxford University Press, New York, 1990.

47 Gaddis, John Lewis, *The United States and the Origins of the Cold War, 1941–1947*, Columbia University Press, New York, 1972.

48 Gaddis, John Lewis, *Strategies of Containment: A Critical Appraisal of Postwar American National Security Policy*, Oxford University Press, New York, 1982.

49 Gardner, Lloyd, *Architects of Illusion*, Quadrangle, Chicago, IL, 1970.

50 Gimbel, John, *The Origins of the Marshall Plan*, Stanford University Press, Stanford, CA, 1976.

51 Griffith, Robert (ed.), *Major Problems in American History since 1945*, D. C. Heath & Co., Lexington, MA, 1992.

52 Gullan, Harold I., *The Upset That Wasn't: Harry S. Truman and the Crucial Election of 1948*, Ivan R. Dee, Chicago, IL, 1998.

53 Hamby, Alonzo L., *Beyond the New Deal: Harry S. Truman and American Liberalism*, Columbia University Press, New York, 1973.

54 Hamby, Alonzo L, *Man of the People: A Life of Harry Truman*, Oxford University Press, New York, 1995.

55 Harbutt, Fraser J., *The Iron Curtain: Churchill, America, and the Origins of the Cold War,* Oxford University Press, New York, 1986.

56 Harper, John L., *American Visions of Europe: Franklin D. Roosevelt, George F. Kennan, and Dean G. Acheson*, Cambridge University Press, New York, 1995.

57 Hartman, Susan M., *Truman and the 80th Congress*, University of Missouri Press, Columbia, MO, 1971.

58 Hastings, Max, *The Korean War,* Simon & Schuster, New York, 1987.

59 Herken, Greg, *The Winning Weapon: The Atomic Bomb in the Cold War, 1945–1950,* Alfred A. Knopf, New York, 1980.

60 Hixson, Walter, *Parting the Curtain: Propaganda, Culture, and the Cold War, 1945–1961*, St Martin's Press, New York, 1997.

61 Hodgson, Godfrey, *America in Our Time: From World War II to Nixon. What Happened and Why*, Vintage, New York, 1976.

62 Hogan, Michael J., *The Marshall Plan*, Cambridge University Press, New York, 1987.

63 Hogan, Michael J., (ed.), *Hiroshima in History and Memory*, Cambridge University Press, New York, 1996.

64 Horowitz, David A. and Peter N. Carroll, *On the Edge: The U.S. since 1941*, 2nd edn, West/Wadsworth, New York, 1998.

65 Huthmacher, J. Joseph (ed.), *The Truman Years: The Reconstruction of Postwar America*, Dryden, Hinsdale, IL, 1972.

66 Isaacson, Walter and Evan Thomas, *The Wise Men: Six Friends and the World They Made*, Simon & Schuster, New York, 1986.

67 Jenkins, Roy, *Truman*, Collins, London, 1986.

68 Jones, Howard, '*A New Kind of War*': *America's Global Strategy and the Truman Doctrine in Greece*, New York, Oxford University Press, 1989.

69 Jones, Joseph M., *The Fifteen Weeks, February 21–June 5, 1947*, Viking, New York, 1955.

70 Kaplan, Lawrence, *The United States and NATO: The Enduring Alliance*, Macmillan, New York, 1984.

71 Kaufman, Burton I., *The Korean War: Challenges in Crisis, Credibility, and Command*, Temple University Press, Philadelphia, PA, 1986.

72 Kepley, David R., *The Collapse of the Middle Way: Senate Republicanism and the Bipartisan Foreign Policy, 1948–1952*, Greenwood Press, New York, 1988.

73 Kirkendall, Richard S. (ed.), *The Truman Period as a Research Field: A Reappraisal, 1972*, University of Missouri Press, Columbia, MO, 1974.

74 Kirkendall, Richard S. (ed.), *The Harry S. Truman Encyclopedia*, Hall, Boston, MA, 1989.

75 Klehr, Harvey, John Earl Haynes and Fridrikh Igorevich Firsov, *The Secret World of American Communism*, Yale University Press, New Haven, CT, 1995.

76 Klehr, Harvey and Ronald Radosh, *The Amerasia Spy Case: Prelude to McCarthyism*, University of North Carolina Press, Chapel Hill, NC, 1996.

77 Knox, Donald, *The Korean War: Pusan to Chosin, An Oral History*, Harcourt Brace Jovanovich, San Diego, CA, 1985.

78 Koenig, Louis (ed.), *The Truman Administration, Its Principles and Practice*, New York University Press, New York, 1956.

79 Kofsky, Frank, *Harry S. Truman and the War Scare of 1948: A Successful Campaign to Deceive the Nation*, St Martin's Press, New York, 1993.

80 Kolko, Joyce and Gabriel, *The Limits of Power: The World and United States Foreign Policy, 1945–1954*, Harper & Row, New York, 1972.

81 Kuniholm, Bruce, *The Origins of the Cold War in the Near East: Great Power Conflict and Diplomacy in Iran, Turkey, and Greece*, Princeton University Press, Princeton, NJ, 1980.

82 Lacey, Michael J. (ed.), *The Truman Presidency*, Cambridge University Press, New York, 1989.

83 LaFeber, Walter, *America, Russia and the Cold War 1945–1992*, 7th edn., McGraw-Hill, Inc., New York, 1993.

84 Leffler, Melvyn P., *A Preponderance of Power: National Security, the Truman Administration and the Cold War*, Stanford University Press, Stanford, CA, 1992.

85 Leffler, Melvyn P., *The Specter of Communism: The United States and the Origins of the Cold War, 1917–1953*, Hill and Wang, New York, 1994.

86 Lehmann, Nicholas, *The Promised Land: The Great Black Migration and How it Changed America*, Alfred A. Knopf, New York, 1991.

87 Leuchtenberg, William E., *In the Shadow of FDR: From Harry Truman to Ronald Reagan*, Cornell University Press, Ithaca, NY, 1983.

88 Liebowich, Louis, *The Press and the Origins of the Cold War 1944–1947*, Praeger, New York, 1988.

89 Lifton, Robert Jay and Greg Mitchell, *Hiroshima in America: Fifty Years of Denial*, G. P. Putnams Sons, New York, 1995.

90 Maddox, Robert J., *The New Left and the Origins of the Cold War*, Princeton University Press, Princeton, NJ, 1973.

91 Maddox, Robert J., *Weapons for Victory: The Hiroshima Decision Fifty Years Later*, University of Missouri, Columbia, MO, 1995.

92 Manchester, William, *American Caesar: Douglas MacArthur 1880–1964*, Little, Brown, Boston, MA, 1978.

93 Marcus, Maeva, *Truman and the Steel Seizure Case: The Limits of Presidential Power*, Columbia University Press, New York, 1977.

94 Markowitz, Norman D., *The Rise and Fall of the People's Century: Henry A. Wallace and American Liberalism, 1941–1948*, The Free Press, New York, 1977.

95 Martin, John B., *Adlai Stevenson of Ilinois*, Doubleday, Garden City, NY, 1976.

96 Mason, Frank, *Truman and the Pendergasts*, Regency, Evanston, IL, 1963.

97 Matusow, Allen J., *Farm Policies and Politics in the Truman Administration*, Harvard University Press, Cambridge, MA, 1967.

98 May, Elain Tyler, *Homeward Bound: American Families in the Cold War Era*, Basic Books, New York, 1988.

99 May, Ernest R. (ed.), *American Cold War Strategy: Interpreting NSC 68*, Bedford Books of St Martin's Press, Boston, MA, 1993.

100 McAuliffe, Mary Sperling, *Crisis on the Left: Cold War Politics and American Liberals, 1947–1954*, University of Massachusetts Press, Amherst, MA, 1978.

101 McCoy, Donald R., *The Presidency of Harry S. Truman*, University Press of Kansas, Lawrence, KN, 1984.

102 McCoy, Donald R. and Richard Ruetten, *Quest and Response: Minority Rights in the Truman Administration*, University Press of Kansas, Lawrence, KN, 1973.

103 McCullough, David, *Truman*, Simon & Schuster, New York, 1992.

104 McKeever, Porter, *Adlai Stevenson, His Life and Legacy*, William Morrow, New York, 1989.

105 McLellan, David S., *Dean Acheson: The State Department Years*, Dodd, Mead, New York, 1976.

106 Messer, Robert L., *The End of an Alliance: James F. Byrnes, Roosevelt, Truman, and the Origins of the Cold War*, University of North Carolina Press, Chapel Hill, NC, 1982.

107 Miller, Merle, *Plain Speaking: An Oral Biography of Harry S. Truman*, Greenwich House, New York, 1974.

108 Miscamble, Wilson, *George F. Kennan and the Making of American Foreign Policy, 1947–1950*, Princeton University Press, Princeton, NJ, 1992.

109 Morris, Richard B. (ed.) *Encyclopedia of American History, Bicentennial Edition*, Harper & Row, New York, 1976.

110 Moskin, J. Robert, *Mr Truman's War: The Final Victories of World War II and the Birth of the Postwar World*, Random House, New York, 1996.

111 Mosley, Leonard, *Marshall: Hero for Our Times*, Hearst, New York, 1982.

112 Newman, Robert P., *Truman and the Hiroshima Cult*, Michigan State Press, East Lansing, MI, 1995.

113   Oshinsky, David M., *A Conspiracy so Immense: The World of Joe McCarthy*, The Free Press, New York, 1983.

114   Paige, Glenn D., *The Korean Decision (June 24–30, 1950)*, The Free Press, New York, 1968.

115   Parmet, Herbert S., *Eisenhower and the American Crusades*, Macmillan, New York, 1972.

116   Parmet, Herbert S., *Richard Nixon and His America*, Little, Brown, Boston, MA, 1990.

117   Parrish, Thomas, *Berlin in the Balance: The Blockade, the Airlift, the First Major Battle of the Cold War*, Addison Wesley Longman, London, 1998.

118   Paterson, Thomas G. (ed.), *Cold War Critics: Alternatives to American Foreign Policy in the Truman Years*, Quadrangle, Chicago, IL, 1971.

119   Patterson, James T., *Mr Republican: A Biography of Robert A. Taft*, Houghton Mifflin, Boston, MA, 1972.

120   Patterson, James T., *Grand Expectations: The United States, 1945–1974*, Oxford University Press, New York, 1996.

121   Pemberton, William E., *Harry S. Truman: Fair Dealer and Cold Warrior*, Twayne Publishers, Boston, MA, 1989.

122   Phillips, Cabell, *The Truman Presidency: The History of a Triumphant Succession*, Macmillan, New York, 1966.

123   Poen, Monte, *Harry S. Truman versus the Medical Lobby*, University of Missouri Press, Columbia, MO, 1979.

124   Poen, Monte (ed.), *Strictly Personal and Confidential: The Letters Harry Truman Never Mailed*, Little, Brown, Boston, MA, 1982.

125   Pogue, Forrest C., *George C. Marshall: Statesman, 1945–1959*, Viking, New York, 1987.

126   Polenberg, Richard, *One Nation Divisible: Class, Race and Ethnicity in the United States since 1938*, Viking, New York, 1980.

127   Powers, Richard Gid, *Secrecy and Power: The Life of J. Edgar Hoover*, The Free Press, New York, 1987.

128   Powers, Richard Gid, *Not Without Honor: The History of American Anticommunism*, The Free Press, New York, 1995.

129   Qingzhao, Hua, *From Yalta to Panmunjom: Truman's Diplomacy and the Four Powers, 1945–1953* (Cornell East Asia Series, No. 64), East Asia Program, Cornell University, Ithaca, NY, 1993.

130   Radosh, Ronald and Joyce Milton, *The Rosenberg File: A Search for the Truth*, Holt, Rinehart & Winston, New York, 1983.

131   Reeves, Thomas C., *The Life and Times of Joe McCarthy*, Stein and Day, Briarcliff Manor, NY, 1982.

132   Rhodes, Richard, *The Making of the Atomic Bomb*, Simon & Schuster, New York, 1986.

133   Rhodes, Richard, *Dark Sun: The Making of the Hydrogen Bomb*, Simon & Schuster, New York, 1995.

134   Ross, Irwin, *The Loneliest Campaign: The Truman Victory of 1948*, New American Library, New York, 1968.

135   Rovere, Richard H., *Senator Joe McCarthy*, Harcourt Brace Jovanovich, New York, 1959.

136 Savage, Sean J., *Truman and the Democratic Party*, University Press of Kentucky, Lexington, KY, 1997.

137 Schaller, Michael, *Douglas MacArthur: The Far Eastern General*, Oxford University Press, New York, 1989.

138 Schaller, Michael, Virginia Scharff and Robert D. Schulzinger, *Present Tense: The United States since 1945*, 2nd edn, Houghton Mifflin, Boston, MA, 1996.

139 Schmidt, Karl M., *Henry A. Wallace: Quixotic Crusade 1948*, Syracuse University Press, Syracuse, NY, 1960.

140 Schrecker, Ellen, *Many are the Crimes: McCarthyism in America*, Little, Brown, Boston, MA, 1998.

141 Sherwin, Martin, *A World Destroyed: Hiroshima and the Origins of the Arms Race*, Vintage, New York, 1987.

142 Skates, John Ray, *The Invasion of Japan: Alternative to the Bomb*, University of South Carolina Press, Columbia, SC, 1994.

143 Smith, John, *Alger Hiss: The True Story*, Holt, Rinehart & Winston, New York, 1977.

144 Smith, Richard N., *Thomas E. Dewey and His Times*, Simon & Schuster, New York, 1982.

145 Snetsinger, John, *Truman, the Jewish Vote, and the Creation of Israel*, Hoover Institution Press, Stanford, CA, 1974.

146 Spanier, John W., *The Truman–MacArthur Controversy and the Korean War*, W. W. Norton, New York, 1965.

147 Steel, Ronald, *Walter Lippmann and the American Century*, Vintage, New York, 1981.

148 Stueck, William, *The Korean War: An International History*, Princeton University Press, Princeton, NJ, 1995.

149 Sugrue, Thomas J., *The Origins of the Urban Crisis: Race and Inequality in Postwar Detroit*, Princeton University Press, Princeton, NJ, 1996.

150 Theoharis, Athan (ed.), *The Truman Presidency: The Origins of the Imperial Presidency and the National Security State*, E. M. Coleman Enterprises, Stanfordville, NY, 1979.

151 Thomas, Hugh, *Armed Truce: The Beginnings of the Cold War, 1945–1946*, Hamish Hamilton, London, 1986.

152 Truman, Margaret, *Harry S. Truman*, Morrow, New York, 1972.

153 Tucker, Nancy B., *Patterns in the Dust: Chinese–American Relations and the Recognition Controversy, 1949–1950*, Columbia University Press, New York, 1983.

154 Tusa, Ann and John, *The Berlin Airlift*, Atheneum, New York, 1988.

155 Ulam, Adam, *Stalin: The Man and His Era*, Viking, New York, 1973.

156 Volkogonov, Dmitri, *Stalin: Triumph and Tragedy*, Grove Weidenfeld, New York, 1991.

157 Walton, Richard J., *Henry Wallace, Harry Truman, and the Cold War*, Viking, New York, 1976.

158 Weinstein, Allen, *Perjury: The Hiss–Chambers Case*, Alfred A. Knopf, New York, 1978.

159 Weinstein, Allen and Alexander Vassiliev, *The Haunted Wood*, Random House, New York, 1999.

160   Whelan, Richard, *Drawing the Line: The Korean War, 1950–1953*, Little, Brown, Boston, MA, 1990.

161   White, Graham and John Maze, *Henry A. Wallace: His Search for a New World Order*, University of North Carolina Press, Chapel Hill, NC, 1995.

162   Whiting, Allen S., *China Crosses the Yalu: The Decision to Enter the Korean War*, Macmillan, New York, 1960.

163   Williams, Robert C., *Klaus Fuchs, Atom Spy*, Harvard University Press, Cambridge, MA, 1987.

164   Wittner, Lawrence, *American Intervention in Greece, 1943–1949*, Columbia University Press, New York, 1982.

165   Woods, Randall B. and Howard Jones, *Dawning of the Cold War: The United States' Quest for Order*, University of Georgia Press, Athens, GA, 1991.

166   Wyden, Peter, *Day One: Before Hiroshima and After*, Simon & Schuster, New York, 1984.

167   Yergin, Daniel, *Shattered Peace: The Origins of the Cold War*, rev. edn, Penguin Books, New York, 1990.

168   Ziegler, Robert H., *The CIO, 1935–1955*, University of North Carolina Press, Chapel Hill, NC, 1995.

INDEX

Page numbers in italics refer to the Documents section.

STUART BRITAIN

Social Change and Continuity: England 1550–1750 (Second edition)
Barry Coward   0 582 29442 8

James I (Second edition)
S J Houston   0 582 20911 0

The English Civil War 1640–1649
Martyn Bennett   0 582 35392 0

Charles I, 1625–1640
Brian Quintrell   0 582 00354 7

The English Republic 1649–1660 (Second edition)
Toby Barnard   0 582 08003 7

Radical Puritans in England 1550–1660
R J Acheson   0 582 35515 X

The Restoration and the England of Charles II (Second edition)
John Miller   0 582 29223 9

The Glorious Revolution (Second edition)
John Miller   0 582 29222 0

EARLY MODERN EUROPE

The Renaissance (Second edition)
Alison Brown   0 582 30781 3

The Emperor Charles V
Martyn Rady   0 582 35475 7

French Renaissance Monarchy: Francis I and Henry II (Second edition)
Robert Knecht   0 582 28707 3

The Protestant Reformation in Europe
Andrew Johnston   0 582 07020 1

The French Wars of Religion 1559–1598 (Second edition)
Robert Knecht   0 582 28533 X

Phillip II
Geoffrey Woodward   0 582 07232 8

The Thirty Years' War
Peter Limm   0 582 35373 4

Louis XIV
Peter Campbell   0 582 01770 X

Spain in the Seventeenth Century
Graham Darby   0 582 07234 4

Peter the Great
William Marshall   0 582 00355 5

EUROPE 1789–1918

Britain and the French Revolution
Clive Emsley   0 582 36961 4

Revolution and Terror in France 1789–1795 (Second edition)
D G Wright   0 582 00379 2

Napoleon and Europe
D G Wright   0 582 35457 9

Nineteenth-Century Russia: Opposition to Autocracy
Derek Offord   0 582 35767 5

The Constitutional Monarchy in France 1814–48
Pamela Pilbeam   0 582 31210 8

The 1848 Revolutions (Second edition)
Peter Jones   0 582 06106 7

The Italian Risorgimento
M Clark   0 582 00353 9

Bismark & Germany 1862–1890 (Second edition)
D G Williamson   0 582 29321 9

Imperial Germany 1890–1918
Ian Porter, Ian Armour and Roger Lockyer   0 582 03496 5

The Dissolution of the Austro-Hungarian Empire 1867–1918 (Second edition)
John W Mason   0 582 29466 5

Second Empire and Commune: France 1848–1871 (Second edition)
William H C Smith   0 582 28705 7

France 1870–1914 (Second edition)
Robert Gildea   0 582 29221 2

The Scramble for Africa (Second edition)
M E Chamberlain   0 582 36881 2

Late Imperial Russia 1890–1917
John F Hutchinson   0 582 32721 0

The First World War
Stuart Robson   0 582 31556 5

EUROPE SINCE 1918

The Russian Revolution (Second edition)
Anthony Wood   0 582 35559 1

Lenin's Revolution: Russia, 1917–1921
David Marples   0 582 31917 X

Stalin and Stalinism (Second edition)
Martin McCauley   0 582 27658 6

The Weimar Republic (Second edition)
John Hiden   0 582 28706 5

The Inter-War Crisis 1919–1939
Richard Overy   0 582 35379 3

Fascism and the Right in Europe, 1919–1945
Martin Blinkhorn   0 582 07021 X

Spain's Civil War (Second edition)
Harry Browne   0 582 28988 2

The Third Reich (Second edition)
D G Williamson   0 582 20914 5

The Origins of the Second World War (Second edition)
R J Overy   0 582 29085 6

The Second World War in Europe
Paul MacKenzie   0 582 32692 3

Anti-Semitism before the Holocaust
Albert S Lindemann   0 582 36964 9

The Holocaust: The Third Reich and the Jews
David Engel   0 582 32720 2

Britain and Europe since 1945
Alex May   0 582 30778 3

Eastern Europe 1945–1969: From Stalinism to Stagnation
Ben Fowkes   0 582 32693 1

The Khrushchev Era, 1953–1964
Martin McCauley   0 582 27776 0

NINETEENTH-CENTURY BRITAIN

Britain before the Reform Acts: Politics and Society 1815–1832
Eric J Evans   0 582 00265 6

Parliamentary Reform in Britain c. 1770–1918
Eric J Evans   0 582 29467 3

Democracy and Reform 1815–1885
D G Wright   0 582 31400 3

Poverty and Poor Law Reform in Nineteenth-Century Britain, 1834–1914:
From Chadwick to Booth
David Englander   0 582 31554 9

The Birth of Industrial Britain: Economic Change, 1750–1850
Kenneth Morgan   0 582 29833 4

Chartism (Third edition)
Edward Royle   0 582 29080 5

Peel and the Conservative Party 1830–1850
Paul Adelman   0 582 35557 5

Gladstone, Disraeli and later Victorian Politics (Third edition)
Paul Adelman   0 582 29322 7

Britain and Ireland: From Home Rule to Independence
Jeremy Smith   0 582 30193 9

TWENTIETH-CENTURY BRITAIN

The Rise of the Labour Party 1880–1945 (Third edition)
Paul Adelman   0 582 29210 7

The Conservative Party and British Politics 1902–1951
Stuart Ball   0 582 08002 9

The Decline of the Liberal Party 1910–1931 (Second edition)
Paul Adelman   0 582 27733 7

The British Women's Suffrage Campaign 1866–1928
Harold L Smith   0 582 29811 3

War & Society in Britain 1899–1948
Rex Pope   0 582 03531 7

The British Economy since 1914: A Study in Decline?
Rex Pope   0 582 30194 7

Unemployment in Britain between the Wars
Stephen Constantine   0 582 35232 0

The Attlee Governments 1945–1951
Kevin Jefferys   0 582 06105 9

The Conservative Governments 1951–1964
Andrew Boxer   0 582 20913 7

Britain under Thatcher
Anthony Seldon and Daniel Collings   0 582 31714 2

INTERNATIONAL HISTORY

The Eastern Question 1774–1923 (Second edition)
A L Macfie   0 582 29195 X

The Origins of the First World War (Second edition)
Gordon Martel   0 582 28697 2

The United States and the First World War
Jennifer D Keene   0 582 35620 2

Anti-Semitism before the Holocaust
Albert S Lindemann   0 582 36964 9

The Origins of the Cold War, 1941–1949 (Second edition)
Martin McCauley   0 582 27659 4

Russia, America and the Cold War, 1949–1991
Martin McCauley   0 582 27936 4

The Arab–Israeli Conflict
Kirsten E Schulze   0 582 31646 4

The United Nations since 1945: Peacekeeping and the Cold War
Norrie MacQueen   0 582 35673 3

Decolonisation: The British Experience since 1945
Nicholas J White   0 582 29087 2

The Vietnam War
Mitchell Hall   0 582 32859 4

WORLD HISTORY

China in Transformation 1900–1949
Colin Mackerras   0 582 31209 4

US HISTORY

America in the Progressive Era, 1890–1914
Lewis L Gould   0 582 35671 7

The United States and the First World War
Jennifer D Keene   0 582 35620 2

The Truman Years, 1945–1953
Mark S Byrnes   0 582 32904 3

The Vietnam War
Mitchell Hall   0 582 32859 4